P9-DET-939

BEING HUMAN:

THE NATURE OF SPIRITUAL EXPERIENCE

BY RANALD MACAULAY & JERRAM BARRS

INTER-VARSITY PRESS
DOWNERS GROVE
ILLINOIS 60515

*InterVarsity Press is the book-publishing
division of Inter-Varsity Christian
Fellowship, a student movement active on
campus at hundreds of universities,
colleges and schools of nursing.
For information about local and regional
activities, write IVCF, 233 Langdon St.,
Madison, WI 53703.*

*Distributed in Canada through
InterVarsity Press, 1875 Leslie St., Unit 10,
Don Mills, Ontario M3B 2M5, Canada.*

*ISBN 0-87784-796-7
Library of Congress Catalog Card
Number: 77-011365*

Printed in the United States of America

To Francis and Edith Schaeffer
who have shown us so much
about serving God and being human,
both in their lives
and by their teaching.

PREFACE

The theme of this book is that understanding the nature of spiritual experience is the key to restoration to true humanness. We believe that teaching on the Christian life should include a strong emphasis on human responsibility and an encouragement to enjoy life.

Some may feel that such a theme improperly emphasizes the "human." Surely a book about the Christian life should be called Being Spiritual *or be focused on the power of God rather than on anything human? It will become clear as the book unfolds that there is no detraction from the Bible's teaching that salvation is initiated and completed by the will and love of God.*

Yet God's desire in delivering us out of lostness into fellowship with himself is to set us free to be human. Being human means being the people he originally intended us to be—serv-

ing him and enjoying him, serving and enjoying each other, ruling and enjoying his good world. Our aim, then, is to lay a biblical foundation for the Christian life on which we hope men and women may labor to construct a beautiful and pleasing building–human life–which will glorify God and endure forever.

As we have talked to individuals and groups over the last few years, we have sensed confusion and uncertainty among many about the Christian life. Some have been maimed by unhelpful teaching. Some have been discouraged after various false starts. Some have been becalmed by an undue emphasis on passivity and have been unsure how to begin again. Others have kept the Christian faith at arm's length because of the negative, antihuman emphasis they have seen. Still others have crashed from a superspiritual high and have wondered whether they can ever pick themselves up again. It is in response to the needs of such people, both Christian and non-Christian, that we have written this book. But we have designed it to be profitable for all believers, young and old, who want to understand more about the Bible's teaching on the Christian life.

It is our hope and prayer that this book will be a help to many and that God will see fit to use it in his kingdom.

HINDERANCES TO CHRISTIAN LIFE

1. UNHELPFUL TEACHING
2. FALSE STARTS
3. PASSIVITY
4. ANTI-HUMAN EMPHASIS
5. COMING DOWN FROM SPIRITUAL HIGH

IN THE LIKENESS OF GOD

ONE

Making simple what appears complicated is one of the marks of a great teacher. Such a teacher was Jesus. When asked what an individual's duty was in relation to the law of the Old Testament, he summarized a vast amount of material accurately and simply:

You shall love the Lord your God with all your heart, and with all your soul, and with all your mind. This is the great and first commandment. And a second is like it, You shall love your neighbor as yourself. On these two commandments depend all the law and the prophets. (Mt. 22:37-40)

Such simplicity does not necessarily involve distortion either. Descriptions need not include every detail to be true. In fact, absolutely comprehensive descriptions which omit no detail are impossible. Yet truth can be known nevertheless: someone did this and not that, was here and not there, was rich and not poor, or whatever.

God's truth makes simple the great range of things which

constitute life, thus enabling us to understand what this
diversity of experiences is all about. That truth is to be found
in God's Word, the Bible.[1]

The Bible itself is not one book, however, but many books;
it covers not one generation, but many. Nevertheless, without denying the wide range of material, we can say emphatically that its basic teaching is simple. And therefore the
simple can read it and "have more understanding than all
[their] teachers" (Ps. 119:99). The fundamentals of the biblical world view are quite straightforward, as we shall see in
chapter two.

Our discussion concerns just one detail within the teaching of the whole Bible, namely, the nature of spiritual experience. What does the Bible teach about a Christian's experience? Again, because there is so much material about
this one subject, we might ask, "Can anything *simple* be said
about it?"

Unhappily, when listening to the various voices in the
church today, one is tempted to conclude no. As in a market-
place on market day, individual teachers and groups are
hawking their own special emphases on the Christian life—
more evangelism, more house churches, more repentance,
more supernatural gifts and so on. This is not simplicity.

This dependence on technique is due in part to our culture's expectation that technology will provide solutions
whenever there are problems. Even the Christian community reflects this mentality: there must be some *technique* which will give the desired solution, fruit, experience,
growth or whatever.

But there is another reason for this confusion. Sometimes
what the Bible says about the Christian life does seem difficult to understand. For example, Jesus says that we cannot
be his disciples unless we lose our lives (Mk. 8:34-35). Paul
says that we have died with Christ and have been raised
with him and that therefore we should "seek the things that
are above, where Christ is, seated at the right hand of God"
(Col. 3:1). What do such expressions as "losing one's life"

and "dying with Christ" mean? Must I have a negative attitude toward life? Does setting my mind on things above mean that I should be unconcerned about present realities?

These passages, when seen in their proper contexts, are not as difficult to understand as they may seem to be initially (see chapter six). Nevertheless, at different times in the history of the church individual statements like these have been picked out of the Bible and misapplied. Very distorted views of the Christian life have resulted.

Is it possible, then, to summarize the teaching in the Bible about spiritual experience? Can it be stated quite simply as Jesus did the law of the Old Testament?

An Organizing Principle

What is needed is what physicists call an *organizing principle*—a principle or law which is so basic to the subject concerned that it controls any future inquiry within it. Starting with such a "control" principle, one is able to explore reality and make new discoveries because of it; yet at the same time one is prevented from adding anything which contradicts it. Has God provided us with such a principle for the Christian life? The question is not whether there is an individual clever enough to formulate such a statement, but rather whether the Bible itself gives us such a key. We feel it does and that it derives, as one would expect, from God's statement concerning man's origin: "Let us make man in our image" (Gen. 1:26).

The choice of this statement as the organizing principle is not arbitrary. The expression *the image of God* means simply "made like God." "Let us make man in our own image, after our likeness" (Gen. 1:26). To say this does not mean that man was completely like God. There were differences of course: man was a limited, physical creature, male and female, who was totally dependent on the Creator not only for the origin of his existence, but also for its continuation. Nevertheless, though unlike God in important ways, man was like God because man was a person.

So the statement, "Let us make man in our image," indicates a completely new step within God's creation. The sun and moon are not his image, nor is the earth, nor are all the creatures that have been created in the air or on the land or in the sea. Only man is described in this way.

The reason becomes apparent within the context of the first few chapters of Genesis: man is made as a creature with whom God himself has a personal relationship. God spoke to Adam and Eve: "Be fruitful and multiply" (Gen. 1:28). They were made so that their ears heard not just sounds, but language. This distinguishes man from the rest of nature. It was natural, then, for them to speak to God: Adam said, "I heard the sound of thee in the garden" (Gen. 3:10). Similarly, it was natural for them to speak to one another and to name the animals (Gen. 2:19).

All the faculties of personality were present in Adam and Eve just as they are present in us. And they are present in us because they were present in them. They were creative and aesthetic, so are we; they loved and reasoned, so do we; they were moral and we are moral; they had choice and we have choice.

This is what likeness to God means, though there is more, as we shall see. Essentially, however, we are like God in that we are persons.

From this truth flows a *definition* of human experience. Like God, we relate to everything personally—he is creative and so are we: we are given dominion over the earth—a dominion intended originally to be benign and so to reflect God's own dominion. We are made also for personal relationships—man with woman, woman with woman, man with man and both with God. These relationships are to be characterized by love in the same way that the relationship among the members of the Trinity is a relationship of love. Therefore, Jesus' summary of the Law and the Prophets, that we are to love God and our neighbor, can be viewed as a clarification of the phrase "image of God" in Genesis 1. The "image" loves because love is of God (1 Jn. 4:7). And the image's purpose is to love. Here is a definition of what it is to be human.

Consequently, we adopt the statement of Genesis 1:26 as the organizing principle first because it speaks of our origin, our very constitution as humans. Second, we adopt it because the New Testament teaches explicitly that the purpose of salvation is to restore this image.

For example, when Paul describes the purpose of sanctification, he says, "Do not lie to one another, seeing that you have put off the old nature with its practices and have put on the new nature, which is being renewed in knowledge *after the image [ikon] of its creator*" (Col. 3:9-10). The use of the word *ikon* is striking. As believers grow spiritually they are being renewed in their Creator's image. "We all, . . . beholding the glory of the Lord, are being *changed into his likeness [ikon]*" (2 Cor. 3:18). In Ephesians 4:24 the term *ikon* is not used, but the idea is the same. "Put on the new nature, created *after the likeness of God* in true righteousness and holiness."

Hence, the purpose of the Christian life, like the purpose of creation, is that we should be like God. Paul reinforces this by saying simply, "Be imitators of God, as beloved children" (Eph. 5:1). Here the likeness is seen by analogy—the child must be like the parent. By imitating God we become like God. The same idea is expressed in reference to Christ. "Be imitators of me, as I am of Christ" (1 Cor. 11:1). It is because Christ is pre-eminently the image of God (2 Cor. 4:4) that we ourselves are to imitate him. We are to "walk in love, as Christ loved us and gave himself up for us" (Eph. 5:2).

John appeals to this also: "If God so loved us, we also ought to love one another" (1 Jn. 4:11). God has acted in this way in Christ because that is God's nature; as John says, "God is love" (1 Jn. 4:8).

The concept of "the image of God" as the organizing principle is specified both in the description of creation, and also in the summary statements of the believer's life in the New Testament.

Sanctification As Affirmation

Sanctification (becoming holy), then, is essentially an *affirmation* of life. The whole purpose of the Christian life is the recovery of the original image of God, in other words, the recovery of the kind of human experience which God intended Adam and Eve to have before the Fall. The Christian experience is not identical to the experience of Adam and Eve, as we shall see. But like theirs, it affirms life.

Ironically, those who stand in the doctrinal tradition of the Reformation and the apostolic church have inherited from the nineteenth century a spirit of negativism quite out of character with these roots. It has been the spirit of "Do not taste, Do not touch" (Col. 2:21). It has been characterized by a denunciation of the mind and a rejection of all cultural activities. The mind has been seen as a boogieman, and creativity as wasteful luxury.[2] And, as in the "tradition" opposed by Paul, this spirit of negativism has been presented as a virtuous and religious attitude.

Over against such a tradition, we contend for a view of sanctification which affirms all those activities which are truly human. Why? Because that is the sort of experience God intended us to have and which he called "very good." As we have seen, Adam was made creative: he named the animals (Gen. 2:19). Also, one of his responsibilities was to "till and keep" the garden of Eden; and presumably he was not insensitive to Eden's beauty. Certainly he was not insensitive to the love he was able to enjoy with his wife. The important point is that we should see just such an experience as fundamental to the Christian life because to be human is to be a reflection, as a finite and physical person, of the experience of the infinite Person who made us.

An Important Distinction

We have been speaking, though, of Adam and Eve before the

Fall. Was this experience not lost irretrievably by the act of disobedience described in Genesis 3?

We must distinguish carefully between what was lost at the Fall and what was not lost. Put another way, we must distinguish between man as the image of God *before* the Fall and man as the image of God *after* the Fall. Those faculties which are peculiarly human, which designate us as persons— love, morality, rationality, creativity—indicate that we continue to be the image of God after the Fall. In this sense, all humanity is, and has been, as truly the image of God after the Fall as Adam and Eve were before the Fall.

Since the Fall, however, these faculties, like eyesight which is impaired, have been defective. It must be stressed, though, that this does not mean that we are no longer human. True, the Bible uses the severe language of "death" to describe our present condition as sinners (Eph. 2:1), but this must not be taken to mean that what we call the human species no longer exists. Humanity is "dead" in the sense of being separated from God; but, though separated, we are still "alive" as humans: we continue to be persons, just as Adam and Eve continued to be persons even when they were expelled from Eden.

This is why we, though fallen, can approach one another as persons. Paul, for example, *reasoned* with the unbelievers of his day, whether Jews or Gentiles. He appealed not only to their minds but to their moral natures as well when he said, "By the open statement of the truth we would commend ourselves to every man's conscience" (2 Cor. 4:2).

This distinction is vital: the image of God remains in us after the Fall, though we no longer reflect God's perfect moral character. Though perfect at the beginning, humanity is no longer so. As we pollute our physical environment, so we pollute our moral environment. We pollute because we ourselves are polluted: "For from within, out of the heart of man, come evil thoughts, fornication, theft, murder, adultery, coveting, wickedness, deceit, licentiousness, envy, slander, pride, foolishness. All these evil things come from within" (Mk. 7:21-23).

In this respect we are unlike God. Nevertheless, it is still legitimate and necessary to speak of fallen humanity as "the image of God," as indeed the New Testament does: "With [the tongue] we bless the Lord and Father, and with it we curse men, *who are made in the likeness of God*" (Jas. 3:9).[3]

First, then, that we are made in the image of God implies an affirmation, rather than a negation of life. Using the analogy of the Israelites when they had safely crossed the Red Sea, we are to view the "land" of the Christian life as Joshua and Caleb viewed Canaan—a land full of beauty and promise. We are not to view it as the other ten spies did— an ominous land, a land that spells fear and bondage. The Christian life should be viewed as life and liberty, recovery and restoration. Too often it has been viewed as a life of dullness and dryness, of repression and rigidity.

A Direction for Life

A second asset of the organizing principle is that it provides us with a direction for life. While sanctification involves an affirmation of life, this does not mean a bare affirmation. Man is not free to do *whatever* he likes. To be made in the image of God is to be made after God's likeness (Gen. 1:26); and the whole of Scripture unfolds to us what such an existence includes and excludes. For example, "Walk as children of light (for the fruit of light is found in all that is good and right and true)" (Eph. 5:8). Conversely, "Fornication and all impurity or covetousness must not even be named among you" (Eph. 5:3). "Be imitators of God, as beloved children. And walk in love, as Christ loved us and gave himself up for us" (Eph. 5:1-2). These wide-ranging directions, both positive and negative, are found within just eight verses of one of Paul's letters. The Scriptures are full of such material.

This is an invaluable asset in the culture in which we live, for people now recognize that they are unable to define life, that, beginning only from ourselves and excluding revelation from God, it is intellectually invalid for finite beings to speak with certainty about truth. Hence the West has been dragged inexorably toward pessimism and moral confusion. As H. J. Blackham says, "On humanist assumptions, life leads to nothing, and every pretence that it does not is a deceit. If there is a bridge over a gorge which spans only half the distance and ends in midair, and if the bridge is crowded with human beings pressing on, one after another they fall into the abyss. The bridge leads nowhere, and those who are pressing forward to cross it are going nowhere. It does not matter where they think they are going, what preparations for the journey they may have made, how much they may be enjoying it all. . . . Such a situation is a model of futility."[4]

Consequently there is an obvious confusion about the way life should be lived—about the moral framework of life. People are directionless. Because they cannot define life, they cannot direct life.[5] Christianity, on the other hand, does both.

Christians claim to know the true meaning of life. This claim is not arrogant. It is based not on Christians' personal authority, nor on their own intellectual ability, nor even on the accumulated intellectual ability of saints and prophets through the centuries. Rather, God, who has revealed himself to man and who has spoken definitively to all people in the Bible, is the sole authority.

The arrogance in fact lies on the other side, with those who refuse to acknowledge that God has spoken. God has made clear the basic things that we need to know about the origin and purpose of life and how life, since the Fall, may now be recovered. Yet many refuse to listen.

So the Bible defines the meaning of life. We were made to be the image of God—to be like God—and this is clearly explained in the directions which the Bible gives concerning what we should and should not do. In a very important sense, then, the Bible is a rule book. Sanctification, as an affirmation of life, is therefore not a call to "do your own thing so long as you do something." The affirmation must be seen within the framework of what God has defined as proper activity, that is, within the limits of the rule book—the Bible.

The Law of Liberty

It is important to note, however, that though the Bible defines what is truly human, the directives for life which flow out of this definition are not to be thought of simply as "rules." There is another whole dimension to be added. The reason the Bible commands and directs is not primarily because it is a *rule* book (though it *is* that), but because it is a *guidebook*. It points us back to the path of life our first ancestors were designed to walk on and which subsequently they left. It identifies for fallen humanity what living as the image of God involves.

Consequently, I look at the admonitions and commands of the Bible not as arbitrary directives, as if God were setting up arbitrary and difficult rules before my stubborn will, like hurdles before a horse in a show-jumping contest. Rather, I see them as carefully chosen directions to lead me back to the path from which sin has beguiled me. I see them as essentially constructive. Why? Because my nature, as created by God, is to live in accordance with such directives. Therefore, when I seek to obey God's commandments, I am not working against myself, but for myself. I am acting in accordance with my nature as the image of God. As I do what is right I establish my true identity: I free myself! Hence Jesus says, "If you continue in my word . . . you will know the truth, and the truth will make you free" (Jn. 8:31-32). And James too speaks of the law as "the perfect law, the law of liberty" (Jas. 1:25).

Having, then, directed me away from the cold atmosphere of negation, the organizing principle profoundly alters my perception of even those things in the Bible which seem at first sight to be negative and restricting. It shows the do's and don'ts to be essentially positive and liberating, for they simply point the way toward the restoration of my true self.

Creativity, Love, Unity

Three aspects of everyday experience throw light on this. The first is creativity. We often think that creativity is limited to those who are specialists in the field, namely, the artists. They are of course specially gifted and have a distinctive role. But in a broader sense, creativity is universal. Every person is an artist. The whole of life is a creative act. The warp and woof of each life is equivalent to the artist's paints or the musician's sounds. We are all weaving—"creating"—life. Because we are made like God, we are real, though limited, "creators."

To say this is not to slight God. Nor is it a humanistic manifesto. We are limited in what we can create, and we continue to sin. Yet even those spheres of life and work considered the most limiting and repressive, like the experience of a slave or a prisoner-of-war, are nevertheless full of creative potential. We may even say that all of us have the possibility of creating with our lives greater works of art than the greatest artists in history, if only because what is created endures. As Jesus said, "If a man remains in me and I in him, he will bear much fruit. . . . fruit that will last" (Jn. 15:5, 16 NIV). And he meant that it would remain into eternity. To say this is not to disparage the work of artists, but to draw attention to the fact that, in a deeper sense of the word *art,* all are artists.

The artist is a person of passion, a person of strong emotion, a person who feels deeply both the tragedy and beauty of life. The artist appreciates shapes, sounds and textures. The artist is a person of action, who selects and molds material and is driven by a sense of excitement at what is involved.

Should not Christians be like this? Should we not be people of passion, in the good sense of that word? The heroes of the faith, like Moses and Elijah, certainly were. Should we not appreciate all forms of beauty? The Psalmist certainly did (Ps. 19:1-4). Like Cowper he "discerns in all things"

A ray of heavenly light, gilding all forms

Terrestrial in the vast and the minute;

The unambiguous footsteps of the God
Who gives its lustre to an insect's wing
And wheels his throne upon the rolling worlds.[6]
Should we not be people of action like Paul who cried, "I have fought the good fight, I have finished the race" (2 Tim. 4:7)?

The artist analogy has much to teach us. In fact every exhortation in Scripture presupposes something like it. Because we are by nature both creatures and creators, we may be exhorted to do various things—to choose to walk according to the Spirit and not according to the flesh, to produce the fruit of light and not of darkness. Sanctification must be seen within the context of creativity. Christians are to take their lives, all their diverse experiences, and mold them into something beautiful, into what the Bible calls "the beauty of holiness" (Ps. 29:2 KJV).

The human ability to love also illustrates the positive character of biblical commands. What is the reason for the Bible's exhortation, "Walk in love" (Eph. 5:2)? Is it that God is love, that Christ is our great example in his willingness to lay down his life for us? Yes, but there is something else as well. We were designed to love. True, there is no explicit statement of this in the Bible. There is no equivalent to John's statement that God is love which says, "man is love." Nevertheless, it is a necessary inference from the fact that we were made in the image of God. Jesus' summary of the commandments presupposes that loving is what human experience is all about.

For this reason the call to a life of love is not arbitrary. The Bible commands it in order to restore our true identity. Therefore, the Bible's exhortation to love and our choosing to love is not a negation but an affirmation of our original nature.

The desire for unity also illustrates the liberating intent of biblical commands. It is one of the outstanding features of history that societies have repeatedly tried to ensure unity. This quest for unity is not due only to some romantic or utopian ideal (even though it is often expressed as such), but to the knowledge deep within us that unity liberates while disunity destroys. Where does this conviction come from? Should we disparage attempts at unity because they are not Christian? Certainly not.

Jesus' final prayer with his disciples was that they might experience unity: "Father, keep them in thy name . . . that they may be one, even as we are one. . . . that they may all be one; even as thou, Father, art in me, and I in thee. . . . that they may be one even as we are one, I in them and thou in me, that they may become perfectly one" (Jn. 17:11, 21, 22-23).

The unity among Jesus' disciples was to be like that among the members of the Trinity—a unity within diversity. In other words, it was a unity which retained the dissimilarity of each individual making up the unit. Just as the members of the Trinity are never to be confused, for each is distinct, so too the proper unity among God's people recognizes diversity. It is the oneness of togetherness, not of singleness.

If, then, we scorn this human desire for unity, we overlook our true dignity, for Jesus' prayer for unity is simply a reaffirmation of the way we were constructed originally. God intended that all people should desire and experience unity. So, even though Jesus' prayer in John 17 is for his people, the church (only a portion of humanity), it is not because he has lost sight of his original vision of a unity encompassing all people, but because some refuse to acknowledge him.

Occasionally we may be right to be skeptical about attempts at political unity and sometimes we may even feel obliged to actively oppose them. But we are never to ignore or disparage them. The cries for unity which come down to us from as far back as Noah's day and the tower of Babel are both pathetic and, at times, reprehensible—pathetic because the unity achieved is always so transient, reprehensible because almost always they are made without regard to the more fundamental issue—unity with God. Yet they are not without their own tragic grandeur. The echo of God's original design is still to be heard in them.

Jesus' prayer for unity and the apostles' frequent exhortations to unity are not merely the application of a legal code. They have to do with the recovery of what was original in Adam. Therefore, to pursue creativity, love and unity is to pursue not just rules for life, but life itself.

Adam and Christ

A very serious objection must now be considered: isn't it a mistake to look back to Adam? Our inheritance from Adam has been evil. Surely the Bible points us away from Adam to Christ?

Certainly the Bible directs us repeatedly and explicitly to look to Christ as both the source and model of life. But there need be no conflict here, for while there are important distinctions between Christ and Adam, there is nevertheless an essential unity between them.

First we must be clear in what ways Christ is to be contrasted with Adam. Paul does this in Romans 5:12-21: through Adam sin and death came upon all, whereas through Christ came the possibility of recovery for all. This is the fundamental difference. In addition, in 1 Corinthians 15:45 and 47 Paul says, " 'The first man Adam became a living being'; the last Adam became a life-giving spirit. . . . The first man was from the earth, a man of dust; the second man is from heaven." This passage indicates the distinction between the human (Adam) and the divine (Christ), the creature (given life) and the Creator (giving life).

Another important distinction appears in 1 Corinthians 15:42-50 between the mortal and the immortal, the perishable and the imperishable. The life which Adam and Eve had was inferior to the life of Christ for their experience was subject to the possibility of mortality: if they took of the fruit of the tree of knowledge of good and evil they would "surely die." By contrast, Paul argues, the new life brought to us by Christ is not subject to death. "Death is swallowed up in victory," that is, in the resurrection from the dead. Therefore Paul says, " 'The first man Adam became a living being'; the last Adam became a life-giving spirit. . . . The first man was from the earth, a man of dust; the second man is from heaven" (vv. 45-47, 54).

Christ came not merely to restore the original, but to bring into existence something different, a human experience not subject even to the possibility of death. It is in this sense that the Bible speaks of Christ's work as a "new creation." So Paul goes on to say that "flesh and blood cannot inherit the kingdom of God, nor does the perishable inherit the imperishable" (15:50). He must not be read here as suggesting that the resurrection is not a physical event, for he has been stressing throughout the chapter that it is. He is simply clarifying that a change will occur in our physical existence at the close of the age—a change from the perishable (inherited from Adam) to the imperishable (inherited from Christ).

So much for the distinctions. What of the essential unity between Adam and Christ? It is the resurrection itself which points this up most clearly, for just as it is human life which is ended by the grave, it is human life in its fullest sense which is restored by the resurrection of the body. It is not a nonhuman or a suprahuman experience which we will enjoy in the future with our resurrected bodies. It is simply a human experience set free at last from the shackles of sin. Some of the experiences we have now we shall have then: we shall see, sing, taste and know. So Paul says, "but then [we shall see Christ] face to face" (1 Cor. 13:12). The apocalypse tells us we shall sing a new song, a song which can be heard (Rev. 5:9; 15:3). Jesus says, "Blessed are the meek, for they shall inherit the earth" (Mt. 5:5). And elsewhere he says (still in the realm of the physical), "I shall not drink again of this fruit of the vine until that day when I drink it new with you in my Father's kingdom" (Mt. 26:29).

These are not references to the unreal or the less real, as if the fully real is only the here and now. The experience of the resurrection, of the life everlasting, even though described by Paul as an experience with a "heavenly body," is still a human experience, and so has a continuity with the experience of Adam and Eve before the Fall, and with ours now.

The point is this: although Christ introduced a qualitatively new creation through his life, death and resurrection, the new was designed to recover the original, not to repudiate it. So the second person of the Trinity became fully human in order to redeem the human, and he remains human throughout eternity. Hence he is called "the last Adam" (1 Cor. 15:45). He is born of woman, as all the descendants of Adam are, and he is truly physical. The recovery of humanity from the effects of the Fall is of such worth to God, that the second person of the Trinity has become human. As such he is our Savior; as such he is our model for the Christian life, not as a type of superman but as an ordinary person. As a son of Adam he was heir to all those experiences which make up human life, except sin. He lived within a family and had special friendships. He entered into the festivities of the wedding at Cana and made it enjoyable through the miracle of his turning water into wine; his enemies even accused him of being a glutton and a winebibber. He was righteously angry as he wept over Jerusalem; he felt compassion for the crowds and exhausted himself in helping them; he sometimes was anxious and distressed.[7]

The distinctiveness of Christ in contrast to Adam must not obscure the essential unity between them as men. Christ certainly was unique, both in his person and in his achievements. His design, however, was the recovery of that same human experience for which he created us originally—fully human, yet without sin.

The reason we stress this is that Christ, not Adam, is to be the center of our lives. Christ is the source of all our spiritual life. Paul says quite simply that Christ is "our life" (Col. 3:4). Moreover, Christ, not Adam, is our model. We are being built up by various means "until we all attain ... to mature manhood, to the measure of the stature of the fulness of Christ" (Eph. 4:13). The focus is to be on Christ.

But we must be clear in what sense Christ is our model. Here is the connection with Adam: the model of the Christian life is the recovery of ordinary human experience— "ordinary" not in the sense of sinfulness, but as opposed to suprahuman; "ordinary" in terms of God's original creation and Jesus' perfect example.

It is neither an ascetic model, nor an eccentric model. The natural, the human, the categories of experience which come down to us from Adam, are all good and are to be received with thanksgiving. Although our natural experiences since the Fall are also the vehicles of sin, the Bible identifies sin as the evil, not the experiences themselves. Just as impurities in water must be filtered out leaving the water itself good, so sin is to be removed leaving the human faculties themselves good.

Equally, the model of "the eccentric" is wrong. Experience does not have to be extraordinary to be charged with spiritual power. Ordinary Christians who are "being renewed after the image" of their Creator will bear the mark of righteousness. That will make them distinctive. The Holy Spirit *may* give extraordinary experiences, both in the area of answered prayer and in the area of spiritual gifts. But we must not construct from these a model for the Christian life.

The natural need not be crushed, nor superseded. It needs to be restored so that it resembles its new Creator, Christ, who in turn resembles Adam before the Fall.

THE BIBLICAL FRAMEWORK AND TWO ALTERNATIVES

TWO

Humanness, being made in the image of God, is like a key which unlocks all the doors in the house of the Christian life. In this chapter we wish to step back from this organizing principle to view the design of the house as a whole. In other words, we intend to examine the framework within which the Christian life is to be understood.

Why is it important to consider this framework? Can we not just get on with considering biblical passages about the Christian life? Why bother with frameworks (biblical or otherwise) and alternative philosophies? These are good questions and deserve an answer.

If the framework within which we consider spirituality is unbiblical, the conclusions we come to about the Christian life and how to grow as a Christian are bound to be wrong. Even if we are influenced unwittingly by unbiblical ideas about the nature of reality as a whole, our understanding of spirituality will be distorted. Some things which are right in themselves will assume a place of importance out of all proportion to their value. Other things which the Bible clearly teaches as of central importance will be given little stress or might even be rejected as having no value at all. To the extent that we are affected by other ideas of the nature of reality, our spiritual experience will be impoverished. Without a knowledge of the "floor plan," we might neglect some rooms, while others, though unlocked and entered, might be misused, and still others disregarded altogether. In ignorance we might even spend much of our lives in imaginary rooms.

So there is a clear need to consider the biblical framework and the alternative views of reality. All teaching on Christian maturity must conform to the teaching of the Bible and its view of reality. The test has to be applied both with regard to content and emphasis. What is taught must not only be true, but properly emphasized.

We will consider three views of reality: the materialistic, the biblical and the Platonic. As we do so we will consider what effects each has on one's view of the Christian life. It should become very clear that it is essential to have the right plan of the house of reality. Distorted ideas about Christian growth can become dominant when the wrong plan or two incompatible plans are used, whether knowingly or not.

The Materialistic View

We live in a largely materialistic culture, a culture which denies the reality of God's existence. Because it denies the existence of God it allows no possibility of the supernatural working into this world. There can be no relationship with God in the present, though psychological techniques may be used to try to give reality a "religious dimension." Further, all life is regarded as the result of the chance process of evolution, producing the present array of diverse forms of life from original matter and energy. Consequently, humans are viewed as an advanced form of animal or as a very complex machine. Each person is regarded as the result of genetic make-up or environmental conditioning or a combination of both. In this view, not only is the supernatural excluded from life, but so is any true human dignity. Our loves, aspirations to heroism, moral judgments, attempts at creativity and even individuality become suspect, having no ultimate value. Because of this view of reality, people seek meaning in the accumulation of material things, in the continual stimulation of the senses and emotions, and in techniques which are supposed to condition them to change.

This materialism has brought about a terrible poverty of human experience in our culture. The old are disregarded because they don't produce sufficiently to make themselves worthwhile units of society. As the spiritual ties which unite families are discarded, the family decays. People increasingly try to find meaning by satisfying their physical and sensual needs. But pleasure and material wealth do not produce happiness or meaning. The stimulation of the senses leads only to the need for greater and greater stimulation till the senses are jaded and unable to appreciate anything. In this vacuum of *human* experience people look desperately for something that will inject meaning into reality. They turn to experience, to the East, to the occult, to the multitude of new religions and new psychologies which spring up day by day.

What does this have to do with the Christian? The materialistic view has rubbed off on the church. Unhappily, the church often reflects society as a whole. Many Christian marriages are ending in divorce. Many Christian homes are little more than passing points for family members who lead totally separate lives. Many Christians become overburdened with the accumulation of wealth and possessions. Others, saddened by this state of affairs, turn to spiritual experiences to try to restore a spiritual dimension to their lives which, apart from attendance at church, differ so little from the lives of non-Christians. Christians sometimes live as practical atheists, professing belief in Christ but without any real conviction that God exists as a person. Without confidence that God exists, the prayer of believers can become sterile. How can I pray, believing that God will answer my prayers by working into this world, unless I'm sure deep down that God is and that he hears?

The materialistic philosophy of our culture creeps in and impoverishes the Christian life in all sorts of ways. Many have grown up in an environment where any supernatural statement of the Bible was explained away. Even if we do not doubt God's existence, we can become like the deist viewing God as the Creator who is removed from this world. Again prayer seems useless.

The Bible's authority is undermined by our culture in every area, whether natural science, social sciences or history. Unless we are convinced that the attacks on the Bible's authority in these areas are groundless, our spirituality will necessarily be affected.

This impoverishment caused by materialism's influence leads to a confusion about what genuine spirituality is. In the search for "life," Christians often turn in the same direction society turns and simply reflect its answers. This "turn" can take two basic directions—either to experience or to techniques.

Just as materially motivated people in our materially motivated society turn to "religious" experiences offered by drugs, Eastern religions and the occult, so Christians too become involved in a frantic search for spiritual experiences which will assure them that God is really there and that they have a relationship with him. Often the experiences sought are valid in themselves, but are given disproportionate importance in proving God's existence and verifying the individual's relationship with him.

Some time ago a girl was vigorously advocating speaking in tongues: "If you get tongues then you'll be really sure of God's love. Then you'll know you have the Holy Spirit's power." A sentence or two later she confessed, "Actually I am about to give up being a Christian. I'm not even sure that God exists or that what the Bible teaches is true." This is very sad. Tongues, which Paul describes as a genuine gift of the Spirit, had become the only nail on which to hang this

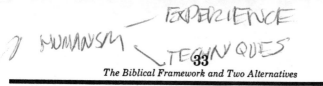

girl's faith, and it could not bear the weight.

Materialism also influences Christians to pursue mechanical techniques as the solution to spiritual weakness. Consequently, much teaching on the Christian life is made up of rules that have to be adhered to.

It is said, for example, that the key to Christian family life is having the right authority structure. Or, it is said that the wife must follow certain rules to keep up her husband's interest—she must remain the "fascinating woman." A list of do's and don'ts show her how. Devotions at a set time each day or reading so many chapters of the Bible a day is said to be the key to a life of prayer. The key to growth is said to be personal evangelism.

Because some churches have been influenced by the moral laxity of our culture and have not practiced biblical discipline, other churches stress discipline and authority so strongly as "the answer" that they give the elders a wider authority over the members' lives than the New Testament suggests. For example, attendance at particular services is made compulsory, people are forbidden to move or marry without the elder's consent, each household must have a particular structure and rules, and so on.

Other proposed techniques concern church health and growth. "What our church needs is an administrative reorganization. Call in a firm of consultants. It will have to be the best. Christ cannot be given second best." That may be and often is one way of trying to deal with the weakness of a particular church. But it certainly will not solve the problems of poverty.

"Our church must have an outreach program. If only we could get everyone involved in evangelism, then the church would grow. There's a new method which has been successful in Los Angeles. Let's try that."

"What we must have is small group Bible studies meeting in homes."

"We need to receive the baptism of the Spirit and speak in tongues, then the church's life can really start."

"Let's have group therapy, then everyone will get to know each other."

"What we need is a larger building in a better situation. Then people will be attracted."

Some of these proposals may have a legitimate place in the life of a church or an individual Christian. Of course there *should* be evangelism, Bible study and spiritual gifts. But how do they come across? New legalisms are set up; a bondage to structures and rules destroys the Christian's freedom. Human relationships and relationship with God are reduced to mechanical patterns. This is the language and method of behavioristic psychology, not of the New Testament!

Techniques do not make a Christian "spiritual" or solve a church's problems for they do not touch the central issues of the Christian life. Only a firm conviction of the truth of Christianity and our commitment to trust and obey God himself, with our minds renewed by the teaching of his Word, will bring any real or lasting change.

The New Testament writers were wise not to set up little patterns or models of how to pray, how to read the Bible or how to evangelize. Each Christian is a unique individual free to work out a pattern of what is most helpful within the framework of the moral law. We are given principles, not techniques.

In evangelism, for example, we are to state the truth plainly, not hesitating to deal with difficult questions (like judgment and the necessity of repentance) lest we scare someone off. We are to witness because we honor individuals as significant and valuable creatures made in God's image who need to hear the truth. Our words must be accompanied, if not preceded, by a life which exhibits the truth of which we speak, a life characterized by love, forgiveness, forbearance, hospitality and compassion. This sort of principle cannot be replaced by techniques or methods however successful. We should not be peddling the gospel with Madison Avenue methods; we should be simply living and proclaiming the truth. The details of how this is done must be worked out in each local situation by each individual or church within the biblical framework.

Humanness, freedom and the possibility of true growth are lost when technique becomes the answer.

The Biblical View

In a sense we should not speak of the Bible's "view" of reality as if it were one alternative among several. For the Bible claims to be *the* truth about the nature of the world in which we live. Its claim to be the truth can be tested and proved, and is exclusive. All other views of reality must be false.

Biblical teaching on the nature of reality begins with God himself. He is the all-powerful Creator of the whole universe and has always existed. Everything else that exists has been made by him at some time in the past. He has always been the same. He did not gradually come into being as the universe grew, nor is he an idea in the minds of men. Rather, all things are dependent on him for their being.

God not only created all things, but sustains all things in their existence. He did not make the world and then leave it, like a watch, to carry on by itself. The laws of nature are in a sense simply descriptions of the way God upholds the universe. He acts into the universe all the time, not just occasionally like some deus ex machina who now and then throws a spear into this world.

God is spirit, not restricted by space and so lives among us, knowing the thoughts and actions of every human being. There is no escape from his presence. Because his knowledge is infinite, nothing surprises him. He is sovereign over the course of this world. He overrules history and some day will bring this age to a conclusion and inaugurate a new age of righteousness.

God is also personal. There are and always have been three persons in the Godhead. God is not some vague spiritual realm or "consciousness," nor is he coextensive with reality, or "all love" or just "being." Rather, the three persons of the Trinity have always existed even before the creation of this world. They loved each other, they communicated with each other. They were morally perfect. They thought and decided and acted on those decisions to create other purely spiritual beings, this material world and also man—a physical/spiritual being. God's own character makes this world a moral world. All things are defined by reference to his character of perfect goodness and justice.

We need to stress that it is not mere metaphor to say that the personal God—Father, Son and Holy Spirit—loves, thinks, communicates, acts, is morally perfect, and creates. These are not metaphors drawn from our own experience by which we attempt to describe a God who is ultimately so transcendent that he cannot be described. They are first true of God himself and therefore are true of us also, as those who are made in his image. We can be described as moral beings, as loving beings, only because God is loving and moral. This is of absolute importance. We are not putting labels on what is really unnamable. Only because God has these personal characteristics do we, made in God's image, have them also. (Interestingly, modern thinkers, having rejected a personal God, are doubtful even about human personality, and so reduce people to machinery simply because they have no ultimate reference point which is personal.)

We were made like God and intended to worship, love and enjoy him. God did not make us to relate to him with one small part of our lives—the spiritual part. He made us to relate to him and express his likeness in all of life—body, mind, emotions, will.

Adam and Eve were made perfect but they chose (and so have we all) to disobey God and to pursue their own way. The human problem since the Fall has been a moral one—rebellion. Our problem is not that we are physical (or mental, emotional or volitional) rather than nonphysical. Nor is it that we are finite, that is, limited to existence in one place at one time, limited to a partial knowledge of reality, limited to knowing the present but not the future. No, there is nothing wrong with humanness as such. Our problem is sinfulness, lack of moral conformity to God's character in every area of life. This has brought sorrow into all our experience. The coming of Christ is God's solution for our sinfulness and its results—pain, confusion, distortion of all of life, and death.

Christ is the second person of the Trinity, the Son. He lived forever with the Father and the Spirit and then at a point in time, in history, was born in Bethlehem. As both man and God, he lived a perfect life. Unlike every other human being there was no moral blemish in his life. He lived in obedience to the Father, and his calling in his life was to reflect God's character. He expressed God's love to us, and had a perfect relationship with the Father. Though as a man he was finite—just as we are—he found this no problem. He was contented to be in only one place at one time, to speak to only one person at a time.

Yet when we examine Christ's life we see him neither using nor advocating any spiritual techniques. His spirituality was expressed in his whole life, not in one little part. When he prayed, he spoke to the Father in ordinary human language. There were no barriers between him and the Father because he was not tainted with sin. The only barrier came when he offered himself on the cross as the substitute in our place, bearing our guilt and punishment. On the cross he experienced physical death and separation from the Father because he was at that point, in one sense, a great sinner and consequently had to bear God's wrath. Hence his cry that he was forsaken by the Father. The sins for which he was punished were not his own but ours. Consequently, as God's righteous Son, he was raised from the grave to live forevermore with a body as both God and man.

We have peace with God and the barriers to a relationship with him are removed if we put our trust in Christ's death for us. If not, we remain separated from God. Because of Christ's work, believers are called God's children. We are indwelt by the Holy Spirit and have a love relationship with

God. This peace with God is the basis on which the whole Christian life is built.

In light of all this, what is our calling as those restored to a relationship with God? Is it to make God present—to "practice the presence of God"? No. Is it to seek spiritual experiences to assure us of his love and power in our lives? No. Is it to pray, to go to church, to study the Bible, to evangelize? No, though it involves these things. Our calling is the same as Adam's was. It is to serve him with our whole life, to love him, to enjoy him, to reflect his character. Every area of our life is to express spirituality, not some special parts of it. Every area of our life in every day is to express the relationship we have with him. Because we have a relationship with him through Christ, we can speak to him simply at any time. We do not have to use any special techniques to make him present or to feel his presence, or to ensure our prayer is real. We can simply talk to him as our loving Father.

Already we enjoy the first fruits of the inheritance Christ has won for us. But we look forward to the day when we shall see him face to face. When we die, though our bodies decay in the grave, we go to be with Christ and we await the day when he will return in power to reign over this earth. If we have died when he comes, our bodies will be raised; if we are alive at his coming, then we will be physically changed and perfected. This transformation at Christ's return is the consummation of our salvation. We will still be finite humans, but we will be without sin and our bodies will no longer be subject to sickness, decay or death. Along with us, the whole creation will be transformed and we shall live in a new earth and heavens, enjoying forever our relationship with God.

The Platonic View
This third view of the nature of reality has had as detrimental an effect on the church as the materialistic view. In some ways it is more dangerous because it can be presented in a way which has a superficial resemblance to the biblical view and for this reason we treat it last. Because of this re-

semblance the Platonic view has influenced the whole history of the church, from the first centuries until today. Therefore, we will trace its ideas and development in some detail. It is important to grasp some of the basic ideas of Platonism, as every Christian meets it disguised in one form or another.

In the Platonic view, reality is made up of two parts—the material realm and the spiritual realm. Figure 1 represents these as two circles. The circles touch but do not overlap, indicating the same about the two realms.

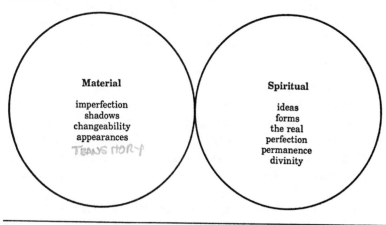

Material

imperfection
shadows
changeability
appearances
TRANSITORY

Spiritual

ideas
forms
the real
perfection
permanence
divinity

Figure 1.

The material realm is the realm of the physical world. It is imperfect, transitory and shadowy. The spiritual realm is the realm of the "ideas," that is, the forms which stand behind the appearances of the material world. The forms or ideas are more real than the things which exist in this material world. The spiritual realm is the realm of permanence, of the perfect, of the real. This spiritual realm is not itself personal, though it may be called divine. The gods may be included in it as spiritual beings.

To understand how this view of reality affects one's understanding of spirituality, let us picture man as another circle, superimposed on the other two as in Figure 2.

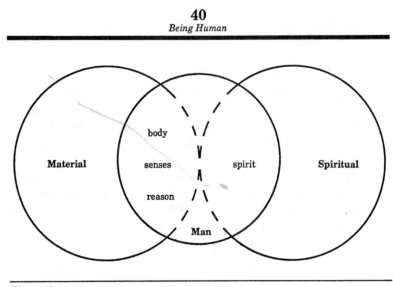

Figure 2.

The Spiritual Is Superior to the Physical

On the one hand, humans are physical and supplied with senses. With our senses we relate to the physical world, evaluating sense perceptions with reason. On the other hand, we each have a spirit. We relate to the spiritual realm through our spirits, not through the senses nor primarily through reason.

Accordingly, in Platonic thought the spiritual realm is considered superior to the material. The spirit is housed in a body of clay from which it longs to be released. Death gives that final release. In this life, however, the aim is to dwell in the realm of the spirit as far as possible and de-emphasize and devalue the material realm. So the philosopher and the artist are those who are in closest contact with the spiritual realm because they are caught up in the contemplation of the ideas, the divine, the beautiful and the celestial.

The material world is not regarded as of no importance. However, it has value only insofar as it acts as a kind of sparkplug to set off the mystical contemplation of the more real spiritual realm. For example, I see the beauty of a flower but I don't "stay" with its beauty. Its beauty is imperfect and I use it only to contemplate the true beauty of the world of the real which stands behind this world. This world has no value, except as a catalyst. Plato says, "He who sees this true beauty is transported with the recollection of *true beauty* when he sees beauty here on earth: *then, careless of the world below....* We see the beauty of this earth and man—a kind of ecstasy overtakes us and the soul is renewed."

Plato has established a spiritual hierarchy. Ordinary people who pursue earthly tasks in the material world are low in the hierarchy because they are not in such close contact with the spiritual realm as the philosopher and inspired artist. Those who have been in contact with the spiritual realm become "careless" of this world. Notice how easy it would be to read the biblical statements against worldliness, or earthly passions or the desires of the flesh in a Platonic way. This would be a mistake.

In his *Phaedrus,* Plato writes of the ways we gain contact with the spiritual realm.[1] He outlines the four ways of "divine madness." By *madness* Plato means that the experience comes from the spiritual realm rather than from or through the mind. The human spirit has direct contact with the spiritual realm. The mind may evaluate the experiences, but the final authority is the divine power or madness which possesses the spirit. The four ways are:

(1) Prophecy. "There is also a madness which is a divine gift and the source of the chiefest blessings granted to men. For prophecy is a madness, and the prophetesses at Delphi ... when out of their senses have conferred great benefits on Hellas; but when in their senses few or none.... Madness is superior to a sane mind ... for the one is *only human* but the other of divine origin."

(2) Healing madness. This seems to be a kind of emotional catharsis caused by contact with the spiritual realm. "Where troubles arise ... there madness has entered ... and by inspired utterances found a way of deliverance for those who are in need ... and he who has part in this gift and is truly possessed and duly out of his mind is made whole and exempt from evil, future as well as present, and has a release from

the calamity which was afflicting him."

(3) Artistic inspiration. Plato makes it clear that there is no entry into the temple of the arts by artistic effort and human creativity. "The sane man disappears and is nowhere when he enters into rivalry with the madman."

(4) Divine love. "The madness of love is the greatest of heaven's blessings." The man of ideas (the one who contemplates heavenly beauty and who knows most of divine love) "forgets earthly interests and is rapt in the divine . . . the vulgar rebuke him and deem him mad . . . they do not see that he is inspired."

In all four of these ways of relating to the spiritual realm there is an emphasis on the uselessness of ordinary human experience. In the presence of the spirit the human is devalued, the mind has no place, creativity is useless, the earthly is forgotten. The spiritual realm is even called the "demonic" by Plato. Socrates, in the *Phaedrus,* hears the voice of the "demonic" within him telling him what he must not do. This inner voice is always to be held as a higher authority than his reason. Because it is from the realm of spirit it must be obeyed.

Platonic Influence on Christianity
Plato's thought had a profound effect on the early church's view of spirituality. In the second century A.D., Justin Martyr had been influenced by Plato before he became a Christian. After his conversion he carried much of Plato's thinking over into his teaching. He called Plato a Christian before Christ.[2] Where the Old Testament was the pedagogue to lead the Jews to Christ, so, for Justin (and later for some of the Greek fathers), Platonic philosophy was the pedagogue to lead the Greeks to Christ.[3] In the next century, Clement and others in Alexandria placed an even greater emphasis on Plato's ideas. The New Testament in particular was read in a Platonic framework. In the third century, Christians began to equate the physical and the sinful completely. Consequently, to obey Paul's command to "mortify

therefore your members which are upon the earth" (Col. 3: 5 KJV), many found it necessary to sit on pillars in the desert or have themselves sealed up in caves!

Plotinus, a third-century Roman philosopher who was not a Christian, is called the father of Neo-Platonism. He elaborated some of Plato's ideas and developed them much further. He stressed the transcendence of the divine, the importance of meditation and the union of the human spirit with the divine in the life of contemplation. He wrote that the way to divine knowledge is "to separate yourself from your body and very earnestly to put aside the system of sense with its desires and impulses and every such futility."[4]

There could be no language about God: "The one is truth beyond all statement. . . . The All-Transcending has no name. We can state what it is not, while we are silent as to what it is. Those who are divinely possessed and inspired have at least knowledge that they hold some greater thing within them, though they cannot tell what it is."[5] This divine encounter was above reason, the mind and feeling. "At the moment of truth there is no power whatever to make any affirmation . . . how is this [the divine encounter] to be accomplished? . . . let all else go."[6]

Plotinus' teaching that religious language is only symbolic was taken up by Dionysius the Areopagite within the Christian church. Dionysius stressed the transcendence (otherness) and oneness of God rather than God's personalness. For Dionysius language about God was meaningless. Verbal prayer was for him only a poor substitute for "real" prayer.

In this connection he is famous for teaching what is called the *via negativa*–the "negative way": Spiritual growth, according to Dionysius, does not come through understanding who God is and what his blessings are. Rather, we must remove all positive statements about God until we are left with silence—the bare communion of the soul with God. Lossky, presenting Dionysius' position, says,

The perfect way, the only way which is fitting in regard to

God, who is of his very nature unknowable, is the second (the negative way), which leads us finally to total ignorance. All knowledge has as its object that which is. Now God is beyond all that exists. In order to approach him it is necessary to deny all that is inferior to him, that is to say, all that which is. If in seeing God one can know what one sees, then one has not seen God in himself but something intelligible, something which is inferior to Him. It is by *unknowing* that one may know him who is above every possible object of knowledge. Proceeding by negatives one ascends from the inferior degrees of being to the highest, by progressively setting aside all that can be known, in order to draw near to the Unknown in the darkness of absolute ignorance.[7]

This emphasis on God being beyond all knowledge is a fundamental characteristic of the mystical tradition of the church. This *way of ignorance* can only be pursued by removing sense and reason, by abandoning not only what is impure but even what is pure. (Later we will discuss the similar emphasis in some evangelicalism of this century on self-emptying, on brokenness, on the uselessness of the mind and doctrine, and on the removing even of what seems good in the self.)

Consequences of Platonic Thinking

The purpose of these spiritual exercises is union with God. The object is to become so united with God in the inner being that one passes beyond subjectivity ("I perceive God") and beyond objectivity ("God perceives me"). The individual attempts to reach a point where the Creator/creature distinction is no longer true or, at least, is no longer perceived.

This kind of union with God is never the purpose of spiritual life in the Bible. There will always be the Creator/creature distinction, even in heaven. When glorified and perfectly restored to God's likeness, we will still perceive God and ourselves as different beings (Rev. 15:3-4; 21:1-6; 19:6-8). Consider Paul's statement: "Then we shall see face to face. Now I know in part; then I shall know fully, even as I am fully known" (1 Cor. 13:12). This is of fundamental importance as we consider what spirituality is. Confusion at this point leads to Watchman Nee's suggestion that our spirit and God's spirit become so one that to us they are indistinguishable and undifferentiable.[8] (In fact it is unhelpful for us to ask whether promptings to righteousness arise from ourselves or from the Holy Spirit implanting his desires within us. But it is unhelpful because his work is secret, not because there is a confusion or merging of his personality and ours.)

The emphasis on the total otherness of God leads to a devaluation of all language and of knowledge perceived by the mind. Language is considered to be essentially idolatrous. "There is only one name by which the divine nature can be expressed: the wonder which seizes the soul when it thinks of God."[9] We have shown elsewhere (pp. 36, 58) that language is not idolatrous because there is a correlation between God and man.

The confusion here arises from forgetting the distinction between true knowledge and exhaustive knowledge, true language and exhaustive language. In saying we can know or say certain things about God, we do not claim that we have said everything about God which can be said, or that we know all that can be known. This is true not only of our knowledge of God but even of our knowledge of other people or of the material world. Though incomplete, our knowledge of God is accurate because he has made himself known to us in the Bible and there described himself for us.

Mystics, forgetting this distinction between true and exhaustive knowledge and stressing that God is utterly different from man, devalued language both as a means of talking about God in theology and as prayer. Notice that neo-orthodox theology is very similar to the mystical tradition at this point. God is considered to be completely other, and so is said to be unapproachable by man. Language about God is thought to be merely an expression of our "encounter" with

God, rather than a true description of him. The Bible itself, it is said, "contains" God's Word and becomes the Word of God only when God is "encountered" in it. Christians must always engage Scripture with the mind and never devalue the mental effort of study with the assertion that Scripture comes alive only when God's spirit "touches" our spirit as we read.

This devaluation of language and mental knowledge makes the Christian life ascetic. The mind as well as everything external is rejected. Sin is said to be "exteriorization," that is, to experience oneself *as a self* is to be in a state of sin. So, there is to be a continuous exodus from oneself. The goal of the spiritual life is to attain to a state of impassibility wherein one is affected by nothing in the external world, or even by any internal passions—a state of quietness beyond suffering or pleasure.[10]

Here, too, there is total confusion about the biblical teaching on what is sinful. It is not the self as such which is a problem, but the sin which affects every part of the self. The sin, not the self, is to be mortified. Evangelicals often become confused about asceticism and the self.

In the mystical tradition, not surprisingly, prayer using words becomes a means to achieve a state of passionlessness. This verbal prayer is said to be only the frontier of prayer. When the state of passionlessness is reached, then begins the wordless, contemplative prayer in which the heart lays itself open before God in total silence.[11] A state of ecstasy is the result, but even this is only the beginning. "The expert," so it is claimed, moves into a state of constant experience of the divine reality.

In order to achieve these states, techniques for prayer are proposed. An example is the Prayer of the Heart—the continual repetition of "Lord Jesus Christ, have mercy on me a sinner." Nicephorus wrote of this prayer:

In every man inner talking is in the breast. For, when our lips are silent, it is in the breast that we talk and discourse with ourselves, pray and sing psalms, and do other things. Thus, having banished every thought from this inner talking (for you can do this if you want to), give it the following short prayer: "Lord, Jesus Christ, Son of God, have mercy upon me!"—and force it, instead of all other thought, to have this one constant cry within. If you continue to do this constantly, with your whole attention, then in time this will open for you the way to the heart which I have described.[12]

But what about Jesus' warning against prayers of vain repetition (Mt. 6:7)? The Prayer of the Heart is really no different from the mantra of Eastern thought.[13] Some Christians use this prayer today, but we should see that the framework in which the use of this prayer and other techniques like it arose, has nothing to do with biblical Christianity. These techniques may certainly produce intense experiences (as does the use of a mantra), but they are quite unrelated to genuine Christian prayer.

Emphasis on this sort of meditation and the mysticism of union with God became, unhappily, a broad stream in the history of the Christian church. The medieval work *The Cloud of Unknowing* betrays in its title the influence of the negative way and of Dionysius. This stream is still with us and its tributaries continue to flow through the evangelical church in unexpected places.

The danger of an uncritical acceptance of this tradition is indicated by some comments of William James in *The Varieties of Religious Experience*. James examines at great length the mystical tradition not only in the Christian church but also in other religions. He comes to the conclusion that all the mystics from whatever source, stand in one tradition. Commenting on the devaluation of language, he points out that if there is nothing to be said, then contrary to the protestations of some of the theologians, doctrine is essentially unimportant.[14]

James also comments that it is odd that evangelicals have abandoned the methodical search for mystical experience and considers that evangelical Protestantism appears flat compared with the mystical tradition. "The naked gospel scheme seems to offer an almshouse for a palace."[15] The "naked gospel scheme" is not an almshouse, however, for the basis of our rejoicing comes not from the pursuit of ecstasy or the experience of the loss of personality in God, but from the knowledge that we who deserve eternal punishment and exclusion from God's presence have been bought back by Christ's death into fellowship with our Creator.

Platonic Thinking Today

Carl Gustav Jung, among the most influential of modern thinkers, stands in the Platonic tradition. His world view is very similar to Plato's. While acknowledging the existence of a spiritual realm, he certainly does not think of the Spirit as the personal God of the Bible. For Jung, Christian doctrine is just one culturally conditioned, verbal expression of the nature of the spiritual realm. Naturally, then, the way of experiencing and describing this reality varies from culture to culture.[16] The Hindu describes this "spirit" in characteristic Hindu terminology; the Muslim in Islamic terms; the Christian in Christian terms. The spiritual reality behind the words is the same.

We should remember, therefore, the use of Christian words is no guarantee that the thinking or the view of reality being offered is biblical. Jung wrote of "God the Father," "Christ" and the "Holy Spirit," but he used these as labels for spiritual experience. The reality behind the words is a vast spiritual realm, but certainly not the personal, triune God of the Bible.

The views of Plato and Jung are being equated by some today with the biblical world view. A striking example is Morton Kelsey.

Kelsey seems to have come from the rationalistic background of modern liberal theology which he rightly considers bankrupt because of its failure to deal adequately with the supernatural element in the Bible. (We will identify the problem of liberalism at a more basic level in chapter seven, pp. 137-39. When confronted by phenomena like dreams, tongues, prophecy and healing, he saw the need to find a framework which accommodated such experiences. He then explicitly adopted the world view of Plato and Jung and equated their view with the biblical world view.[17]

According to Kelsey, the main human problem is not moral, but is the need to be in contact with the spiritual realm. His central emphasis is not the atonement of Christ, but spiritual experiences which, he says, are the means by which one is restored to contact with the spiritual. Consequently, he stresses tongues, healing, emotional catharsis, spiritual filling, meditation, prophecy and dreams. The Spirit brings wholeness primarily in these ways. The *extraordinary* becomes the Spirit's *usual* way.

Kelsey acknowledges that when one makes excursions into this spiritual realm of the unconscious one is opening oneself up to evil as well as good and so one needs a spiritual confessor to guide one through these dangerous waters. This realm (which he refers to as the Holy Spirit or self) is a place of subconscious forces or spiritual powers beyond our normal rational experience. A journey into it is intended to restore a lost dimension to our experience parched by materialism and thus revitalize our lives. This thinking is very similar to the gnostic theosophies which plagued the early church and is right in line with the resurgence of interest in religious experience and the occult which exists in our culture. What is particularly dangerous about Kelsey's thinking is that it is presented in biblical language.

Nevertheless, this is not biblical Christianity. The acknowledgment of a spiritual realm and the use of God's names to describe it do not mean that a biblical view is present. The Holy Spirit is not "a spiritual realm," nor is he the unconscious part of our psyche, nor the spiritual ground of all human life. He is not a part of any of these things. The Holy Spirit is a personal being. And we come into a relationship with him not through extraordinary spiritual experiences, nor through meditation, nor inward silence, but through believing that Christ died for our sins. Therefore, spirituality is to be expressed not by the sort of "divine encounter" which Kelsey, Jung or Plato suggest, but simply by loving the personal God who made us and redeemed us, and by obeying his commandments.

We stress this because Kelsey's book *Encounter with God* already seems to have confused many true Christians to the point of believing that biblical Christianity is what Kelsey describes. For instance, one prominent charismatic leader is quoted on the cover: "Kelsey's book . . . points people to a discoverable reality . . . it could have, in the field of theology, the kind of effect that Copernicus had in the field of astronomy—it sets forth a whole new scheme of reality. It provides the most thoroughly worked-out and documented theology for the charismatic which has been done anywhere. Beyond this it offers a whole new perspective from which to teach the Christian faith. . . . I'd love to see it used as a textbook."[18] In the foreword of the book another charismatic leader writes: "It gives encounter an undergirding of theology."[19] Though *Encounter with God* was considered to be one of the most important books of 1974 by evangelical leaders in England (in a survey conducted by *Crusade Magazine*), we feel that the theology undergirding the encounter has very little similarity with biblical theology.

It is naive to think that Christ is honored wherever the Holy Spirit is mentioned or "experiences with the Spirit" are encouraged. The New Testament commands us to test spiritual claims by biblical doctrine (1 Jn. 4:1-3; Gal. 1: 6-9).

Platonists Unaware
Morton Kelsey is an example of one who has deliberately adopted elements of the Platonic world view. More frequently, someone within the mainstream of orthodox Christianity is influenced by Platonism without realizing the source, and genuinely confuses it with biblical teaching. For example, extraordinary spiritual experiences may be consid-

ered ultimate (rather than subordinate) in the Christian life, or the mind may be devalued.

Watchman Nee provides several clear examples of this kind of Platonic influence. According to Nee, the person is composed of three parts: the inner man (the spirit), the outer man (the soul) and the outermost man (the body). Because they belong to the outer man, neither the emotions nor the mental thoughts have the same nature as God. Only the spirit relates to God.[20] Nee seems to say that the spirit of the Christian and God's Spirit are fused. The self, or soul, must be broken for the spirit to be released.

Nee's stress on dependence on God, and on the humility we ought to have as sinners is of great value. But it seems to us that he goes beyond this valuable emphasis when he speaks of the breaking of the soul to release the spirit. He seems to be rejecting not merely the sinful nature but the self, for is not the self constituted by the emotions, the mind, the will— Nee's "outer man"? Consequently he devalues the human. He says that natural compassion and tenderness are still sinful because they are only human. These too must be broken to allow the Spirit to do his work.[21] This breaking of the self he regards as a particular experience which one must seek to have.[22]

Nee says, further, that to read the Scriptures with the mind is not enough, even though we may think we have been helped.[23]

Nee's teaching in these areas may flow from a misunderstanding of Galatians 2:20: "It is no longer I who live, but Christ who lives in me." This, he seems to have taken to mean that the self must no longer play any part in the spiritual life, the "I" must be replaced by Christ. This is why he sees all the efforts of the self in attempting to practice righteousness as sinful. This also explains his view of the necessity of enlightenment, as over against mental effort, in reading the Scriptures.

What does Paul mean in Galatians 2:20? He cannot be taken to mean that the self is or must be replaced, for he goes on to add in the same verse: "The life I now live in the flesh I live by faith in the Son of God, who loved me and gave himself for me." Paul's "I" continues to live—it has not disappeared and should not disappear. Further, the context indicates that Paul is dealing with the question of justification through faith alone. In verse 19 he says, "I died to the law": Paul is no longer trying to justify himself or build himself up. Rather, he is "living to God." His life is now centered on God and thankfulness to him. Verse 20 simply reiterates the same point. He is no longer trying to establish his own righteousness before God or with no help from God. Instead, he sees Christ as the source of his whole life. Christ's work is now central to his existence.

Paul recognizes that without Christ he would be "dead"—alienated from God. Only through his faith in Christ is he alive to God, and therefore truly alive. Christ has brought light to his mind; where before he was ignorant of the truth, now through Christ he has wisdom. Where before the need to justify himself brought rebellion against the law and bondage to sin, now because of Christ he is free to obey the law and to practice righteousness.

As Paul looks at himself, he sees that his whole life as a believer is built upon the foundation of Christ's work. Faith in Christ is the central ingredient of his relationship with God, of his relationships with others and of his own inward security. Because of this continual state of dependence on Christ, Paul can make the startling statement: "It is no longer I who live, but Christ who lives in me." Paul is no longer living autonomously. He knows that his life flows from Christ, his Creator and Redeemer. But Paul is not making a statement of nonexistence of the self, nor of self-rejection.

Much of what Watchman Nee has written is very helpful, particularly his emphasis on faith and the need to be yielded in all things to God, but his teaching on the self is unbalanced, unhelpful and contrary to the New Testament's teaching.

Physical for Eternity

The biblical view of several areas, particularly the body, the world, spiritual gifts and prayer, is worth noticing in relation to Platonic thought. The Bible's view of the body is quite different from the Platonic view. God called his *physical* creation "very good." Our physical nature is part of our structure as human beings. Because our bodies are made by God they are to be enjoyed. Consider the celebration of sexuality in the Song of Solomon. We are called to honor God in our bodies (1 Cor. 6:20) and to offer our bodies as living sacrifices to God (Rom. 12:1-2). Paul here uses the term *body* to refer positively to the whole "self" in somewhat the same way that he uses the term *flesh* to refer negatively to the whole of our "sinful nature."

The great value God gives to the body is best shown by the physical resurrection. We will be physical for eternity. The passage which may seem most Platonic, at a superficial glance, is in fact the very opposite of Platonic thinking (2 Cor. 5:1-5). In this passage Paul speaks of his longing to be released from this life and from this body which is subject to mortality. We long, however, not to be "unclothed, but that we would be further clothed, so that what is mortal may be swallowed up by life." Paul longs not for a *less* physical experience but for a *better* physical experience—one unmarred by sickness and decay.

In fact, Paul adds that the Holy Spirit is given to us as a guarantee of this physical resurrection. Far from being unspiritual or having nothing to do with true spirituality, the body is of such supreme value to God that we are given the Spirit to assure us that we always will be physical. He puts the same great emphasis on our future physical life in Romans 8:23 where he equates our adoption with the redemption of our bodies. Thus asceticism for its own sake has no place in Christianity.

Separation of Sacred and Secular

Platonism, as we have seen, teaches that as we become absorbed in the spiritual realm "we become careless of the world below." Is this what the New Testament means when it urges us not to love the things of this world?

The "world" in the New Testament is the sphere of life in which God's lordship is rejected, where the things of this life become ends in themselves or even are worshiped. The world in this sense is most certainly to be rejected, but this does not mean that we are to hate life, culture, nature, sex and other material things. "Everything created by God is good, and nothing is to be rejected if it is received with thanksgiving" (1 Tim. 4:4). Paul even asserts that the teaching that the material world is not to be enjoyed is a doctrine of demons (v. 1). We have been created to enjoy God's world in all its richness. Human culture is also to be enjoyed (see chapter six).

Spirituality involves the whole of human life; nothing is nonspiritual. But wherever Platonism has affected Christian teaching there has been a separation of the sacred and secular. Thus, prayer, worship, evangelism and "the ministry" are thought to be sacred. All other activities are secular. The sacred is said to be more spiritual.

Even where a necessary involvement in everyday tasks is acknowledged to be a Christian duty, the work, it is said, has to be done only physically.[24] The spirit within has to be involved in silent communion with God, practicing his presence. This is similar to the command of the *Bhagavad-Gita* to act as if we were not acting, love as if we were not loving.[25] The necessity of involvement in the world of people and things is accepted, but the action must be done with the spirit withdrawn into the secret place of union with God, where the "real" business of life is said to be carried on.

This mentality subtly affects Christian thinking in numerous ways. For example, someone might say, "If only I could be involved in something really spiritual like witnessing rather than peeling these potatoes." The New Testament stands absolutely against this division of life into more and less spiritual sections. Consider Ephesians 5:18. We are commanded to be filled with the Spirit continuously. How is this to be expressed? In singing psalms and hymns and spiritual songs; in giving thanks in all things; and also in thinking of others' needs as we submit to one another in the ordinary everyday relationships of husband and wife, parent and child, employer and employee. We are to obey God's Word in all these areas, living before him in dependence on his Spirit. This is what it means to be filled with the Spirit.

Paul says elsewhere that we are to do everything in the name of the Lord Jesus Christ (Col. 3:17). All we do is to be done under the lordship of Christ—even washing floors. Everything we do as human beings is spiritually important. There is no sacred and secular.

This does not mean merely that we see practical value in "secular" tasks like peeling potatoes and washing the floor. It means far more: God himself delights in them because he has created the realm of the physical. Therefore, we are to value every part of our lives just as he does. In fact, spirituality is to be expressed primarily in the ordinary everyday affairs and relationships of our lives. God will reward his servants both for their work in everyday tasks (even if in slavery—Col. 3:22-24), and for their work in proclaiming the gospel (1 Thess. 2:19). Anything done well on the foundation of Christ will be approved by God on the day of the believer's judgment.

Gifts: No Natural/Supernatural Division

Associated with this scorn of mundane activities is the devaluation of natural, as over against supernatural matters. Platonic thinking separates that which is merely human from that which is spiritual, the mental from the divine.

The same kind of division is made by Christians in the area of gifts: the natural and the supernatural, the ordinary and the charismatic. But, is this a biblical division? In the New Testament's teaching on gifts there is no such division made between the human and the divine. Gifts as varied as teaching, prophecy, service, encouraging, contributing to the needs of others, leadership, showing mercy, speaking with wisdom, speaking with knowledge, faith, healing, miraculous powers, distinguishing between spirits, tongues, interpretation of tongues, apostles, helping others and administration are all called charismatic in 1 Corinthians 12:8-10 and 28-31, Romans 12:5-8 and 1 Peter 4:10-11. In each of these four passages in the Greek text the term *charisma* (literally "grace gift") is used. (Though *charisma* is not used in Eph. 4:7-11, we might also add evangelism and pastoring to the list. Marriage and singleness are also referred to as *charismata* in 1 Cor. 7.)

It is plain that the various lists include both "ordinary" and "extraordinary" gifts, but no division of natural/supernatural or human/divine is indicated. It is wrong to label particular gifts extraordinary and say these are the *really* spiritual ones. That a gift like tongues or healing or working miracles is more obviously given directly by the Spirit, does not put it on a higher plane. Nor does it demonstrate that the person who exercises such a gift is more open to the Spirit or knows a fullness of the Spirit not enjoyed by others who have more ordinary gifts.

Singling out the extraordinary gifts is not necessarily expressing greater openness to the Spirit: it may in fact define the work of the Spirit too narrowly. The Spirit works into the whole of our lives, in our ordinary human experience as well as in extraordinary ways. The Spirit was involved in the creation of each of us; he has been the sovereign Lord over each of our lives; he has given us new life as believers; he gives us new gifts after we become Christians, either "ordinary" or "extraordinary."

Jeremiah, for example, was prepared from the womb for his calling as a prophet of God. His whole life contributed to make him God's prophet. This was true also of Paul. When Paul became a Christian, God added gifts to those he had already given him at birth which had been developed by his training. All these worked together to make Paul, the apostle, God's gift to the church. The same is true of each one of us.

On the other hand, the "extraordinary" gifts should not be devalued. That would be as mistaken as the disproportionate value sometimes given to them. We should all desire good gifts and believe that God will give them to us, ordinary and extraordinary, when his church needs them. For example, if we are faced with someone who has been into the occult or the demonic, we should pray for the gift of discernment or that Satan will be restrained in order that the person may be able to believe, or if necessary we should exorcise in the name of Christ. God forbid that any of us should be antisupernaturalists. Let us not become practical atheists.

At the same time, we should see that the Spirit works into our whole lives, not just into a narrow, "spiritual" area. To use one's mind in teaching does not mean that the result is unspiritual or that no charismatic gift is being exercised. We should not set the human and the divine in opposition. The Spirit works in dramatic and obvious gifts, and equally in less obvious and less dramatic gifts.

Prayer

As we have seen, in the Platonic tradition within the church, nonverbal ecstatic prayer was considered the highest way. Meditation and other techniques were practiced to bring the soul into a state of realizing God's presence. Prayer was viewed as a way of experiencing the Spirit's presence within. But what is prayer? Is the meditation that the Bible speaks of, the meditation of the Prayer of the Heart that we considered earlier? Is it a method for practicing God's presence?

Occasionally the psalmist is said to meditate on God's wonderful works or God's character. He recalls the way God has delivered his people in the past and this gives him confidence to pray in the present (Ps. 77:12; 143:5). But the word *meditation* is principally reserved for the consideration of God's law. Joshua is commanded to meditate on the book of the law day and night (Josh. 1:8); and it is a frequent refrain of the psalmist that the righteous man so loves God's law that he meditates on it continually (Ps. 1:2; 119:15, 23, 48,

78, 148 and others). The nearest parallel in the New Testament to this idea of meditation is in Colossians 3:16: "Let the word of Christ dwell in you richly."

Notice, then, how different from the meditation of the mystical tradition is the meditation encouraged by Scripture. It is obviously the opposite of the "negative way" for it is a meditation rich in content. It is not the emptying of the mind, but the filling of the mind. The believer meditates on God's Word, seeking to know both what God has commanded in Scripture and how this is to be applied.

Biblical meditation is not intended to make God present. God *is* present with the believer and therefore the purpose of prayer in the Scripture is to communicate to God in ordinary language one's praise, thanksgiving, confession, troubles and requests. Because God is personal and uses language himself, ordinary human language is a perfectly good medium for communicating with God. God is not the absolute other. Language is not valueless to describe God, nor to speak to him. Sometimes, of course, we may feel so troubled about a particular issue which faces us or so confused about how to pray in some situation that we cannot find words to express ourselves. Then the Spirit, who knows the deepest needs and desires of our hearts, prays for us (Rom. 8:26-27).

Further, the reason for praying is not to experience God or to feel God's presence, nor is prayer meaningful only when there is such a feeling. The Apostle Paul says simply, "Do not be anxious about anything, but in everything, by prayer and petition, with thanksgiving, present your requests to God" (Phil. 4:6).

So, prayer need not be complicated, beautifully expressed or extraordinary in any way. Nothing could be more simple than the model prayer which Jesus taught his disciples (Mt. 6:9-13; Lk. 11:2-4). Even for the second person of the Trinity, ordinary language was adequate to communicate his deepest needs and greatest longings to his Father.

This is not to say that prayer is or should be without emotion. As we pray we ought to be overwhelmed with thanksgiving for God's love in giving his Son for us; we ought to grow in our appreciation of God's character. As with our Lord, deep emotion may indeed accompany our prayers and be the result of them. "And the peace of God, which passes all understanding, will keep your hearts and your minds in Christ Jesus" (Phil. 4:7). The presence of God with us and his love for us are the factors which encourage us to pray—they are never the end toward which we pray.

Concerning the things we have just examined, the biblical teaching at each point stands opposed to Platonism, however diluted. There is simply no warrant in Scripture to devalue the human or the natural. Materialism is equally to be avoided. God desires that men and women be fulfilled in every aspect of their humanness as they grow day by day into the likeness of himself, enjoying fellowship with the living God.

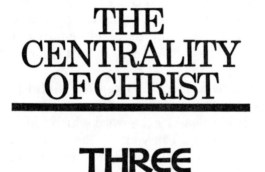

THE
CENTRALITY
OF CHRIST

THREE

Before continuing our discussion, let's look back over the terrain we have covered. In chapter one we argued that restoration to the image of God is the organizing principle of the Christian life. Next we stepped back to view the entire framework of the Christian life and, in particular, to see how the body, the world, gifts, prayer and spirituality fit into that design.

Having identified the goal of the Christian life as restoration to the image of God and having seen that this involves an affirmation of human life, the next question is, how can this restoration be achieved?

We have already said that our problem is a moral one. The reflection of God's character has been marred by sin—sin which alienates us from God. No human effort can please God sufficiently, for all have failed to reflect his character perfectly. By his unerring obedience, however, Jesus Christ became the new man, the second Adam, who did reflect God's image perfectly. By this perfect obedience to God and by his death as our substitute, he has made us acceptable to God.

Now, restored to a right relationship with God our Creator through trust in Christ, we must seek to be like him, who is the very image of God. But *how* shall we become like him? *How* shall we be restored to God's image? Simply by trying to live as Christ did? No. Christians must actively follow Christ's example, but our problem remains. Though accepted in Christ the beloved, we are still sinners. As Luther said we are *simul justus et peccator* ("we are justified and at the same time sinners"). Given our sinful nature, how can we ever change? Jesus himself gave us the answer: "You are already made clean by the word which I have spoken to you. Abide in me, and I in you. As the branch cannot bear fruit by itself, unless it abides in the vine, neither can you, unless you abide in me. I am the vine, you are the branches. He who abides in me, and I in him, he it is that bears much fruit, for apart from me you can do nothing" (Jn. 15:3-5).

Only as we look to Christ in confidence and are thankful for all *he has done for us* is there any possibility of growing into his likeness. Change does not come automatically when we have once believed, nor does it come easily, but the beginning point for growth, the motivation for change, is simply our trust in Christ and our gratitude for all he has done for us. "Beholding the glory of the Lord, [we] are being changed into his likeness from one degree of glory to another" (2 Cor. 3:18).

Two false paths to maturity must first be eliminated before we examine in detail the correct one. In his letter to the Colossians, Paul speaks of two types of spiritual teaching which also are prominent in the church today. Colossians is a masterwork on the centrality of Christ, and was written to counter a brand of teaching to which some modern thinking is nearly equivalent.

Though it is difficult to say precisely what the false teaching was, Paul's warnings indicate two main elements.

Asceticism

The first false path is asceticism. Certain physical and ceremonial regulations had to be observed by the Christian in order to grow—fasts, diet, physical techniques and the observance of certain religious festivals (Col. 2:16-23). These ascetic regulations aimed to restrict or restrain the body as if this would enable the Christian to become truly spiritual. They may have thought, "If I can control my body by subjecting it to a rigorous diet, by treating it harshly, by doing exercises to gain control over it (observing set times and days for prayer and religious observance), then I (my spirit) will be free from the passions and lusts of the body, free from the controlling power of sin, able to be truly mature as a Christian. I will be on a higher plane, unaffected by the normal demands of life and the various temptations to sin."

Concerning this false teaching Paul says, "Let no one pass judgment on you in questions of food and drink or with regard to a festival or a new moon or a sabbath. . . . Why do you submit to regulations, 'Do not handle, Do not taste, Do not touch!'?" (2:16, 21). He also refers to harsh treatment of the body (2:23).

This problem has arisen again and again in the history of the church—and still exists today. Every few years a new brand of asceticism raises its Platonic head and claims to be the key to Christian spirituality. As a way to become spiritual through restraining or controlling the body, some Christians encourage yoga. Though yoga springs from Hinduism (a totally unbiblical framework) many say it is a neutral technique—that helps one to become more devoted or single-minded in prayer. Through yoga, they say, one is freed from the usual cares and temptations of the body and mind, enabling the spirit to approach God unhindered.

Transcendental meditation is another practice sometimes advocated by Christians in order to give renewed concentration in prayer and freedom from external concerns. This way, it is suggested, life goes on as usual, yet the spirit of the meditator remains unaffected, quiet in communion with God.

Certain foods are said to inhibit the spiritual life. Meat, for example, is said to make one feel heavy so that the mind and spirit are not liberated, making prayer more difficult. The practice of interior silence is advocated so that "the spiritual life can flow unrestricted in me and I can hear the spirit's voice." We are told we can learn from the East's spirituality even if we reject its basic teaching of pantheism.

Along with Eastern mysticism there is a growing reverence for the mystical tradition in the church's history, particularly that of Eastern Orthodoxy, but also of Catholicism and Protestantism. Morton Kelsey's *Encounter with God* is an example (see pp. 48-50). When Kelsey discusses Christian growth, he lists a dozen ways Christians can grow— the practice of introversion, inward silence, recording dreams, fasting, depth psychology and others. The rules for achieving spiritual encounter are "much like the practical ones athletes must follow; they are empirical rules for spiritual training."[1] Concerning "the practice of silence and introversion," he comments:

> The practice of introversion is probably the most basic and fundamental rule of the spiritual encounter. It is the process of turning in upon one's self and away from the material world of people and things, and this is the germ of prayer, the beginning of communion with the non-physical world. Without the practice of introversion there can be no real growth in the realm of the spirit. Until we turn our backs on the outer physical world, we cannot become free of the idea that there is really nothing special within man. Only as we do turn away from the material world does the world of inner reality come before us. It is in this inner world that we have direct experience of the spirit and receive its power.[2]

Notice the emphasis here. Though not explicitly ascetic, the language is the same—rules for becoming a spiritual athlete, the rejection of the external material world, the emphasis on spirituality being an internal thing rather than relationships with other people, the direct experience of the Spirit in one's inner world, and the impersonal "its" referring to the Spirit. The basic idea in Kelsey's suggestions is the same as that in the Colossian false teaching: regulations release the spirit from the external world of people and things.

Paul's verdict on this kind of teaching is worth quoting in full.

These [regulations] are all destined to perish with use, because they are based on human commands and teachings. Such regulations indeed have an appearance of wisdom, with their self-imposed worship, their false humility and their harsh treatment of the body, but they lack any value in restraining sensual indulgence. (Col. 2:22-23 NIV)

The goal of the Christian life is to be restored to God's likeness, to be holy as God is holy, to be like Christ in character. It is not primarily to have direct experiences of the spirit or to become a kind of spiritual athlete. Consequently, Paul says, these regulations imposed by the Colossian teachers and their contemporary counterparts have nothing whatsoever to do with genuine Christian growth and true spirituality. They are of no value in restraining the desires and practices of the sinful nature.[3] These techniques and regulations arise from Platonism and the world view of the East where the goal of spirituality, union with the spiritual realm, is a consequence of turning away from the external world of people and things. The biblical goal is holiness of life, expressed primarily in the giving of ourselves in service to other people. Paul's condemnation of the Colossian heresy could not be stronger. These regulations have no value in the Christian life.

This must be our response to anyone advocating yoga, diet control, transcendental meditation or fasting as a means to control the body and mind, or any special religious observances as the way to spiritual maturity. Even if they seem to be of spiritual value they are of no value whatsoever because they involve a complete misunderstanding of what the Christian life is all about. They do not help at all in growing in one's relationship with God or in controlling sin. They do not improve the value of one's prayers in any way. In chapter two we saw that as Christians our starting point for prayer is that we *already* have a relationship with God through Jesus Christ. We don't have to do anything to get into God's presence, or to make him present or to give our spirit free reign. Through Christ he has become our Father and he simply promises to hear us when we come to him in Jesus' name.

(There is, of course, a legitimate place for fasting in the Christian's life. The Bible encourages us to set aside time from the demanding schedule of our lives including the time spent on preparation and eating of meals when there are matters of particular importance for which to pray. Fasting is to be regarded as an indication of our earnestness in prayer or repentance and must be matched by an earnest attitude of heart. But fasting is not to be regarded as a virtuous activity which puts God into our debt so that he is more likely to answer our prayers. Nor must it be seen as a rule, the keeping of which prepares us for "real" spiritual service. When it becomes either of these it deserves the same condemnation as God pronounced when Israel regarded religious ceremonies in this way [Is. 1:11-17; Ps. 50:8-15; Hos. 6:6] or the scorn Jesus poured on the legalism and self-righteousness of the Pharisees [Mt. 23:23-24].)

Another variation on the "rules and regulations" approach toward the Christian life is widespread today. Though not produced by the influence of Platonic thinking, these "rules" can be equally misleading about genuine spirituality. They spring from a legalistic mentality and generally take one of two forms. First, there are the negative regulations about lifestyle which are considered the mark of the Christian who is not ashamed of his testimony: don't drink, smoke, dance, go to movies or wear certain clothes. Second, there are the positive regulations held to be the measure of spirituality or the way to maturity: read so many chapters of the Bible a day, pray for so long, witness to so many people a week.

By saying that such rules are often unhelpful, we are not

commending drunkenness or discouraging Bible reading, prayer or witnessing. The lists of rules and regulations by which Christians are sometimes required to live, however, are a poor substitute for true spirituality. Often they are counterproductive—creating a bondage to human regulations (specifically condemned by Paul in both Col. 2:23 and Gal. 3:2; 5:1) and fostering rebellion.

A false notion of spirituality is inculcated when people feel they are spiritual—that they have a "good testimony"— simply because they have obeyed the rules. For it is possible for anyone to stop smoking, drinking or going to the movies. By an exercise of the will, anyone can fulfill little rules about prayer and Bible reading and witnessing. But emphasis on these (and fulfillment of them) may obscure the demands of God's law and the individual's real lack of conformity to it. To love God with all your heart, and your neighbor as yourself and to "do justice, and to love kindness, and to walk humbly with your God" (Mic. 6:8) is quite a different matter than to obey certain rules.

Equally detrimental to spiritual growth are the guilt feelings fostered when the Christian does not pray, read the Bible and witness as much as the "regulations" specify. The very rules which were intended to be helpful cause frustration, bondage and ultimately a dread of the mention of "devotions" or "quiet time." How different from the delight the Christian ought to have in prayer and Bible study.

"Higher Spirituality"

The second element of the false teaching in Colossae concerned an emphasis on a "higher spirituality"; and here again we see a remarkable similarity to the church today. Paul says, "Let no one disqualify you, insisting on self-abasement and worship of angels, taking his stand on visions, puffed up without reason by his sensuous mind" (Col. 2:18).

The members of the Colossian church were being made to feel unspiritual and to doubt the reality of their relationship with God by people who insisted that they themselves were on a higher spiritual plane. The Colossians had been taught originally that their whole Christian life was built upon their confidence in Christ, that in him they had received every spiritual blessing. The false teachers undermined this confidence by insisting that without certain spiritual experiences the Colossians could not be truly mature. Paul warns: "Don't let anyone put themselves on a higher level and you on a lower level because they think they have entered into some deeper spirituality, because they claim to have been initiated into mysteries."

The false teachers demanded that all should abase themselves, and thereby open themselves up to these special experiences, without which their spirituality was suspect, second class, inferior. Paul's phrase, translated "taking his stand on visions," was a technical expression in the first few centuries A.D. which has been found on temple inscriptions.[4] It refers to the way of entering into a "higher spirituality." Those who "took their stand on visions" had been initiated into particular experiences of either Gnosticism or the mystery religions by a "spiritual encounter." This is similar to "receiving knowledge" as taught by the Divine Light Mission today.

Paul also refers to abasing the self. The false teachers were saying that the "self" must be broken so that one could be open to the spiritual experience and thus enter "the higher level." Paul regarded this self-emptying as the opposite of true humility—pride. Nothing could be more opposed to true spirituality.

Though these teachers thought they had access to a special, higher spirituality, in fact they were elated or puffed up without reason by their sinful minds. True spirituality results in a walk before God and other believers which is characterized by humility, a sense of sinfulness and weakness, and an awareness of the poverty of one's own spirituality. Jesus was referring to this attitude when he said, "Blessed are the poor in spirit" (Mt. 5:3).

This "Colossian pattern" is often repeated. Someone will say to a Christian, particularly a young Christian or one in difficulty, "This is good, you've believed in Christ. But now, in order to show that you really have a relationship with God and are really living a spiritual life, you must experience...." Depending on who is speaking, the blank will be filled with speaking in tongues, the baptism of the spirit, the second blessing, brokenness or what have you. The spiritual counselor continues: "Then you will be sure of the Spirit's indwelling and have power. You will be able to witness and pray freely. Then you won't just *believe* that you have the Holy Spirit in you, you'll *know by experience*."

The result of this is exactly as Paul describes. The Christian is disqualified, robbed of assurance in Christ, and made to feel unspiritual, unfaithful and in need of something extra—something more than and higher than the cross. This is invariably the case if the person happens to be introspective or subject to depression. Often the one "pushing" the experience will create an even greater sense of insecurity and need with questions calculated to cause lack of confidence: "Are you living victoriously?" "Do you feel weak and unspiritual?" "Are you sure the Holy Spirit is dwelling in you?"

This approach is very destructive because it robs the individual of true Christian assurance—confidence not in self or in any feeling, but in Jesus Christ and his atoning death. True, today, as in Colossae, a place is given to Christ and his work; but by stressing a higher spirituality beyond faith in Christ, this teaching implies that Christ and his death are only the gateway to a superspirituality. This can hardly be opposed too strongly. For, as Paul says, it denies that Christ's work on the cross is the necessary *and sufficient* basis for maturing as a Christian.

Grace Is Sufficient

By this strong statement, we are not warning against the use or enjoyment of spiritual gifts, whether "ordinary" or "extraordinary." We should exercise and encourage others to exercise whatever gifts we or they have. We must not quench the Spirit (1 Thess. 5:19), but be thankful for any gift which is being used in a biblical manner and with a biblical emphasis. However, if extraordinary gifts are overvalued and seen as the gateway into, or the mark of, a higher spirituality, then Paul's criticism of the Colossian false teachers applies.

Moreover, we are not warning against particular experiences individual Christians may have. We are not trying to devalue anyone's experience. Experiences that build faith, whether dramatic or undramatic, are to be received gratefully. The key question is: What is central or essential in the Christian life?

It is instructive to note what Jesus said to his disciples after he had sent them out to preach the gospel, to heal and to cast out demons. Returning to Jesus the disciples were overwhelmed with joy because they had cast out demons in his name. But Jesus said, "I saw Satan fall like lightning from heaven. . . . Nevertheless, do not rejoice in this, that the spirits are subject to you; but rejoice that your names are written in heaven" (Lk. 10:17-20). The point Jesus emphasizes here is that though it is wonderful and exciting to use the gifts God has given us and to see victories against Satan, these things must never become the central factor in our lives. Always at the center must be our rejoicing because of God's unmerited love toward us—that we, though sinners, though worthy of condemnation, have been saved for eternal life with God because of the work of Christ on the cross. This is to be the basis for rejoicing, for growth, for maturing as Christians.

Another place where the same point is made is in 2 Corinthians 12. Paul, defending himself against the unjust attacks of the false apostles, speaks of the visions and revelations he has received from the Lord (12:1). He has "heard things that cannot be told, which man may not utter" (12:4). But he goes on to say that in order "to keep me from being too elated by the abundance of revelations, a thorn was given me in the flesh, a messenger of Satan, to harass me. Three times I besought the Lord about this, that it should leave me; but he said to me, 'My grace is sufficient for you, for my power is made perfect in weakness' " (12:7-8). The idea here is the same as in Colossians. God didn't want Paul to be conceited, puffed up by this experience. God didn't want this to become the center of Paul's life as a Christian, lest he feel he was more spiritual than others. Paul gives thanks for his visions, but he realizes there is a danger in such experiences. He was given a thorn in the flesh to remind him always that the basis for his rejoicing must be God's grace expressed in Christ's work.

Clearly, then, Paul is not warning against experiences that come from God and are sanctioned by the Bible. Nor are we. What we *are* warning against (as did Paul) is the dividing of the Christian community into two levels on the basis of particular experiences which some Christians may have had. Paul rejects such an idea absolutely. Our maturity and rejoicing must be based simply on Christ's work for us.

What is the antidote to such false teaching? Since Christian maturity means being like Christ, we must look to him. He is the new man. He is the one whose love motivates us to change and the one who is the model for change. In Colossians, Paul emphasizes that all growth comes through appreciating the wealth of Christ's love for us. It is striking that in a letter dealing with Christian maturity, Paul concentrates almost exclusively on Christ's person and work. If we look in some detail at his teaching, we will see why.

First, Paul writes of Christ's supremacy over the whole creation. Christ is Lord of all, the Creator of everything that has been made, both visible—the world of matter, plants, animals and humans—and invisible—the world of the angels and spirits (1:15-16). He has always lived and he sustains in existence the whole of created reality (1:17). He is also the supreme Lord of the church, both because he is himself God (1:19) and because of his death and resurrection (1:18). "We proclaim him, counseling and teaching everyone with all wisdom, so that we may present everyone perfect [mature] in Christ" (1:28).

Aiming more particularly at the false teaching, Paul states that in Christ "are hidden all the treasures of wisdom and knowledge" (2:3). Therefore he says, "Let no one deceive you by fine-sounding arguments." He continues in 2:6-7—"So then, just as you received Christ Jesus as Lord, continue to live in him, rooted and built up in him, strengthened in the faith as you were taught, and overflowing with thankfulness." But, he warns them, "See to it that no one takes you captive through deceptive philosophy.... For in Christ all the fulness of the Deity lives in bodily form, and you have this fulness in Christ, who is the head over every power and authority" (2:8-10; references in this paragraph and the preceding are from the NIV).

All maturity in the Christian life flows from Christ because he is fully God and because he has died for us. Because of this, Paul proclaims only Christ both to the unbeliever and the believer. He *never* goes beyond Christ. He does not say that the *beginning* of the Christian life is faith in Christ and accepting his work in thanksgiving, and that *fullness* in the Christian life comes through a higher experience such as being "baptized in the Spirit." Here, where Paul is dealing with the question of how to become mature as a Christian, he refers to the Spirit only once (1:8). Why is this? It is because the Spirit's work is to glorify Christ, to take what is Christ's and declare it to us (Jn. 16:14). Therefore, there is no greater evidence of the Spirit's work than the extolling of Christ.

Elsewhere Paul says that as we behold Christ we are changed from glory to glory into the same likeness, and this is the work of the Lord who is the Spirit (2 Cor. 3:18). Of course it is important to speak of the Spirit and his work explicitly, but it is a mistake to think that there is no true spirituality, that the Spirit is not being honored or that the Spirit is not working except when he and his gifts are specifically referred to.

Gratitude and Growth

Paul insists that Christians have already come to fullness of life simply through faith in Christ. We will continue to grow as we understand and are thankful for Christ's work. Without gratitude for Christ's death there will be no change and no possibility of change. Thanksgiving is fundamental.

Why is thankfulness the basis for change? Because it alone can soften our hearts which are so rebellious toward God and his law. In appreciation for God's mercy to us in Christ, we are to give our lives to serve and obey God. Paul says, "I appeal to you therefore, brethren, by the mercies of God, to present your bodies as a living sacrifice, holy and acceptable to God—which is your spiritual worship" (Rom. 12:1). To the elders in Ephesus he said, "I commend you to God and to the word of his grace, which is able to build you up and give you the inheritance among all those who are sanctified" (Acts 20:32).

Thankfulness points us away from what we have achieved or failed to achieve and makes us focus instead on God's love, which alone can warm our cold hearts and set them on fire with delight in God and in serving and obeying him. If we look only at our own efforts, we soon become overwhelmed by our failures and sink beneath the waves of discouragement. If we look only at any minor successes or at any experiences we may have had, we easily become proud and again there is a block in the way of loving God (1 Pet. 5:5).

As only the love of Christ can constrain us to change our sinful attitudes and habits, it is of fundamental importance that we understand what Christ has done for us and what our salvation cost him. Just as a person saved from drowning is thankful, so should we be when we understand our deliverance by Christ. This is why Paul in the Colossian letter dealing with Christian growth, spells out so carefully who Christ is and what his work has accomplished.

To the extent that we forget that our status before God is due to what Christ has done for us, we will try to make our own relationship with God depend on winning his approval.

Thinking that unless we fulfill certain obligations God will not love us, we begin to focus on what we have or have not done. We make an anxious search for internal evidences of our "new life." But doubts arise as to whether God really loves us. Then, as we realize we cannot possibly meet his standards, resentment builds up against God for making such strict demands. So our hearts gradually harden against him and obedience becomes more difficult. Joy, wonder and praise dry up. Instead, frustration and a sense of failure make us feel empty and sterile.

If we get in this state what should we do? It is often at just this point that superspiritual teaching or some kind of second blessing emphasis may gain a foothold. Certainly the Christian life should not be sterile and joyless. Should we begin to search for some "higher" spiritual experience? No. Rather than seeking for something else, we should turn back thankfully to Christ and remind ourselves of who he is and what he has done for us. Ingratitude eats away at one's whole life by producing spiritual drought and bitterness.

On the other hand, one's own imagined spiritual maturity and achievements can produce ingratitude that is expressed as spiritual pride. This pride drowns all sense of need for deliverance from this "body of death" and is complacent in the face of inability to measure up to the standards of God's law. We start to think we have made it; we are more critical of others and less critical of ourselves. Centering on Christ can alone motivate us to love and obedience; centering on ourselves produces bitterness or complacency. Knowing this, Paul points the Colossians to Christ's work for them.

Reconciled to God
Paul first outlines the effect Christ's death has on God's attitude toward the believer. "And you, who once were estranged and hostile in mind, doing evil deeds, he has now reconciled in his body of flesh by his death in order to present you holy and blameless and irreproachable before him" (Col. 1:21-22). This means that God has been propitiated by the

death of Christ on the cross or, in other words, that God's anger against our sin has been turned aside through Christ.

We often forget this; we think that all we must do is say "sorry" to God and he will forgive us. But apart from Christ's death, our apologies would not turn God's anger from us. Paul emphasizes that we are estranged from God and are his enemies, apart from faith in Christ's atoning death.

This alienation is inevitable, given our sin and God's perfect moral character. Because he is just and good, even the slightest wrongdoing on our part creates a chasm, both in the present and for eternity, between him and us. One who breaks the law at one point is guilty of all (Jas. 2:10). In fact, of course, all of us have broken the law at many points and continue to do so. God judges our wrongdoing, and so we become his enemies. This was our position before we believed in Christ, and would be our position now apart from his death for us. Of ourselves we could do nothing to bring about a relationship with God.

It is important to see Christ's work against such a backdrop of our estrangement from God. Otherwise, we will be thinking all the time that there is something we must add, something we must do, something else we ought to experience, in order to come to a full relationship with God. The Bible says there is only one thing that saves us—Christ's work.

When Christ died on the cross, he dealt completely with the barrier between us and God. Being God and perfectly righteous, his death was sufficient to bear the judgment due to us, so that God could be reconciled to us. On the cross, Christ became a curse and, dying, suffered separation from God the Father. Therefore, when we put our faith in Christ, God is able to have a relationship with us and adopt us as his children. Apart from Christ's death we would have nothing to look forward to but eternal exclusion from God's presence.

Rescued from Darkness
Paul also views the work of Christ in its effect on the princi-

palities and powers of darkness. "He has delivered us from the dominion of darkness and transferred us to the kingdom of his beloved Son, in whom we have redemption, the forgiveness of sins" (Col. 1:13-14). We think of Satanists and occult practicers and those involved in explicitly demonic activities as belonging to Satan's kingdom, but we tend to see the rest of mankind, including ourselves before we were Christians, in a neutral position—hovering between the two kingdoms. However, the New Testament teaches that there are only two possibilities: either we have fellowship with God and through faith in Christ are in his kingdom or we belong to Satan. There is no neutral ground. Jesus called Satan the prince of this world, the world to which we belong. So every individual who is not a believer is a member of his kingdom. Satan is even called the god of this world by Paul. Humanity lives in enemy-occupied territory, and we are all subjects of its king.

Satan can claim all human beings as his subjects because of our sinfulness and because, being made in God's image, we have a moral nature. We all do wrong, and we know it is wrong. We all make moral judgments—"he ought to have helped with the dishes," "she made an unkind remark." Our thoughts are full of this kind of judgment of others. Every time we make a judgment we approve God's law, we acknowledge that the commandments are right. When we condemn unkindness in someone else, we are approving the law that commands kindness—likewise across the whole spectrum of the law of God.

It is as if we autograph God's law every time we make a moral judgment. We add our signatures to the law in approval. Paul makes this point most fully in Romans 1 and 2, and in Colossians 2:14 he refers simply to the "written code, with its regulations, that was against us and that stood opposed to us" (NIV). Paul is referring to God's moral law which we have autographed, acknowledging its distinction between right and wrong and, by implication, admitting that we are worthy of condemnation if we ourselves do what is wrong.

Satan's power over sinners is this very document. The principalities and powers of darkness use God's law—which we have signed—as evidence against us in the court of heaven. The devil can say, "This man is mine! He broke the law. He agreed that breaking the law deserves judgment. See his signature. The case is proved. He is my subject!"

But that is not the end of the matter. Paul points out that Christ triumphed over Satan (Col. 2:14-15). Christ has taken away Satan's power against us in that he nailed that document to the cross and bore its curses and sanctions. Our adversary, Satan, no longer has any claim against us. Having borne our punishment, Christ ransomed us at the cost of his own life from Satan's kingdom. Satan can no longer condemn us or claim us as his own.

Furthermore, belonging to the kingdom of darkness means that there is no neutrality in any area, not even in the area of ideas. So whatever religion or philosophy we consider (Buddhism, Hinduism, Islam or simply atheism or humanism) is on the side of Satan and belongs to his kingdom.

This is what Paul is saying when he refers to the *stoicheia* ("basic principles") of this world (Col. 2:8 NIV). This Greek word has several meanings: (1) the basic physical elements of earth, air, fire and water; (2) the basic principles of life, of human philosophy; (3) the elemental powers behind the course of this world which is in rebellion against God. Therefore, to be taken captive by non-Christian philosophy is to be taken captive by "the authorities . . . the powers of this dark world" (Eph. 6:12 NIV).

There is no neutrality in the battle between the kingdoms. Whatever our thinking was previously, we were outside God's kingdom and in Satan's. As unbelievers we were not only subject to Satan's moral accusations, but also to his delusions in the area of ideas. In this too, however, Christ triumphed over the principalities and powers. Since he led these powers in a triumphal procession when he died on the cross (Col. 2:15), and since they had to acknowledge him as Lord and conqueror when he died on our behalf, they were made impotent before him.

Consequently, we need no longer be held in thrall to false ideas and ignorance. Christ has shone into our darkness. Through him we are truly free to be members of God's kingdom. We are free to grow in our understanding of the truth, no longer bound by a non-Christian philosophy which could never give enlightenment, provide meaning or impart life. We are free to enjoy our new citizenship in the kingdom of God's beloved Son.

Renewing the Mind

Paul also views the work of Christ in its effect on those who have believed in Christ. We have passed from death to life, and, indwelt by the Holy Spirit, we have a new relationship with God as his children. This is a reality, no matter how we may feel, no matter how hard pressed we may be. We have already been adopted into his family.

It is in regard to this new status that the New Testament speaks of remaking or renewing the mind. Paul writes that we are to be transformed by the renewing of our minds (Rom. 12:2). In Colossians 3:1-2, before he spells out obedience in the Christian life, Paul says, "Set your minds on things that are above, where Christ is, seated at the right hand of God." Paul is calling us to focus our minds on our new status in Christ because the more we realize what this status is and the more we are thankful for it, the more we shall be encouraged to obey.

Notice the Bible's emphasis on the mind, a subject we will be taking up at length in a later chapter. Often the mind is devalued and said to have little place in Christian growth. Watchman Nee wrote: "We must recognize two very different ways of help for us. First there is a way which seems right in which help is received from the outside through the mind by doctrine and its exposition; many will even profess to have been greatly helped this way; yet it is a help so very different from that help which God intends."[5] Nee then says that the right help is God's Spirit touching our spirit. There is a quite unnecessary division here between the work of the Spirit and the place of the mind, between doctrine and internal experience. Paul says that using our minds to understand the doctrine of our status before God is basic to Christian growth, and Peter writes, "Prepare your minds for action" (1 Pet. 1:13).

The Spirit works into our minds and our ordinary human experience, using our understanding and developing a new mindset in order to build us up and sanctify us. The Bible says, in fact, that his chief work is to take the things of Christ and to help us to understand them. I need not *feel* the Spirit touching my spirit, flashing on like a light bulb in my head or heart as I read the Scripture. God promises that as I acknowledge Christ's lordship, depend on him and pray, his Spirit will work into every area of my life. As we seek to understand the Bible with our minds and to see more clearly our privileged position as believers, the Spirit helps us grow. Because the work of Christ is actual, because he died and rose again in history, this is not just positive thinking or a psychological technique. It is reality.

But when Paul calls us to set our minds on things above, not on things on the earth (Col. 3:2), is he describing a new flight from the material world around us, from the world of people and things, from our everyday environment? What does Paul mean by "earthly things"? In the New Testament, *earth* and *world* often refer to the world as it is characterized by rebellion against God and as it is affected by sin, the curse and judgment. Paul is demanding that we no longer see life from such a perspective, from the perspective of our lives before we became Christians. Rather, we are to have the perspective of our new status in Christ. We are to remind ourselves, for example, that no matter how we may feel at a particular moment, no matter how discouraged, how weak, how subject to sin, how alone, in fact we belong to God who loves us because of the work of Christ. We are to set our minds on things above "where Christ is seated at the right hand of God."

Beloved Children

This means first that we are accounted with Christ as God's beloved children. Since Christ is our representative, what he achieved he achieved for us: "One has died for all; therefore all have died" (2 Cor. 5:14). When he rose, he rose for us. We are united with him in his death and resurrection. Because Christ gave himself to death on our behalf, God exalted him and gave him a name above every other name (Phil. 2:9). He is the beloved Son with whom the Father is well pleased and he is now seated at the Father's right hand. Being united with him in his death and resurrection, we too are God's beloved children. We are sons and heirs with Christ (Rom. 8:17).

Just as Jesus is regarded with favor and honor by the Father, so are we. Now that Christ has removed our sin and the alienation caused by it, there is no barrier to our fellowship with God. We are God's children who may call him "Daddy," "Father," with no fear of rejection. Our being received by the Father with favor is as certain as Christ's being received by him. Count Zinzendorf expressed it this way:

Jesus, thy blood and righteousness
My beauty are, my glorious dress,
Midst flaming worlds, in these arrayed,
With joy shall I lift up my head.

Such is the assurance of acceptance believers in Jesus may have—even though the world burns in judgment we need not fear the fire.

There is, therefore, no barrier to our prayers. With Christ at God's right hand we have immediate access to his presence. We are his beloved as Christ is his beloved. We are his elect who belong to him (Col. 3:12). We no longer belong to the world of sin and rebellion which, under Satan's rule, is passing away. Our citizenship is in the kingdom which is coming and will fill the whole earth when Christ returns. We are in that kingdom already, enjoying the privileges and honors as members of it. We are all kings with Christ. If you are tempted to be depressed, if you feel guilty or discouraged, overwhelmed by failures and mistakes, if ill health or anxiety is dragging you down, it is very easy to forget God's love and to feel rejected and unworthy. But we are to remember what our position is as God's beloved children and be thankful. We are to set our minds on this.

In addition Christ has been placed far above all other powers and authorities of this age and of the age to come, and he is the one who is victorious over all, who is King of kings and Lord of lords for the church (Rev. 19:10; Eph. 1:21-22). Yet Christ is in this position of great authority as our representative who speaks and acts on our behalf. He said, "All authority in heaven and on earth has been given to me" (Mt. 28:18). This authority is for us. From this position of power he has poured out his Spirit on us who have believed. The Spirit has given us new life already and will continually give us power and strength to change. In each one who believes in Christ the Spirit is present with this power from Christ who is at the Father's right hand.

When we are weak, beset by temptation, wondering how we can continue to struggle against sin, we are to recall Christ's position of power and remember that he is there for us, and that if we ask for the help of his Spirit he will never refuse. In fact, it is only as we see our weakness and inability in the face of sin and temptation and Satan's enmity that dependence on God becomes meaningful and we realize how much we need God's grace and power. That is why Paul says God's power is made perfect in our weakness, and "I will all the more gladly boast of my weaknesses, that the power of Christ may rest upon me" (2 Cor. 12:9). Until we recognize our weakness and poverty in ourselves, we do not realize how much we need the blessings which flow to us from Christ's work. Then, in thankfulness we call out to God to deliver us, and to strengthen us inwardly by his Spirit.

New Life with Christ
So we have been reconciled to God, rescued from Satan's

dominion, our minds are being renewed and, above all, we enjoy all the privileges of God's adopted children. This is all part of our new life in Christ. Our old life is finished. "You have died, and your life is hid with Christ in God" (Col. 3:3).

But exactly what does this mean? Some claim that something inside us as believers actually changes or a part of our person, "the spirit," which before was dead is made alive, and so we can look inside ourselves and see "a new life" there. Paul does say that we are a new creation, that we have new life, but he does not mean by this that a dramatic change, observable internally, has taken place in some part of us. He is referring, primarily, to our new status before God: because Christ is our representative and is alive, we too, being *in* Christ by faith, have life. Before faith in Christ, we were dead in the sense that we could not have fellowship with God because of our sin. When we believe, because our guilt is covered by Christ's death, we have a new life, that is, we are alive to God and now have fellowship with him. Death and life in this context do not refer to the nonexistence of the self or a part of the self (say, the spirit), but to the status of an individual before God—either dead (because under the judgment of sin) or alive (because *in* Christ and therefore accepted by God).

The new life we have is ours because Christ is our representative. We do not have to *feel* new. Very often in fact we are painfully aware of how much our old life is still with us. Our new life is only partially enjoyed at present because it is "hid with Christ." We will enjoy it to the full when we are completely new within—only when Christ returns. Until then, we are to grasp in faith the truth that because we are united with Christ, God treats us as his beloved children. Newness, then, though not yet fully experienced, is already a present possession.

Because we belong to Christ, we can even say that the new creation within us is our *true* identity. With Paul we can say, "It is no longer I . . . but sin which dwells within me" (Rom. 7:20). Paul is not excusing his sinfulness, as if there were some other person inside him—not Paul—doing the wrong. He is simply pointing out that his *new* identity in Christ is his *true* identity. The sin which is still very much with him will not be with him permanently. The new, sinless Paul will prevail. He already has a new desire to do right, created by the Spirit, so he longs for the unveiling of his true self at the resurrection. Being a new creature in this sense, Paul is encouraged to do battle with his sinful nature.

The Weight of Glory
Finally, since Christ is our representative, the glory which he already experiences will be ours also. This is both a spur and a comfort to us when we are discouraged. Just as Christ was raised bodily from the dead, so will we be raised in order to enjoy his presence face to face. We have a hope which is not simply wishful thinking, nor against all the evidence, but which is based on something completely objective—the historical resurrection of Christ.

Therefore, when Christ appears in glory, we will appear with him. It is right to focus on the glorious revelation of the Lord when we think of Christ's return. But, remarkably, the New Testament also refers to our own revelation in glory. We too will have a glorious unveiling (Col. 3:4; Rom. 8:19). We are to set our minds on this so that we may endure difficulty, because, as Paul said, "This slight momentary affliction is preparing for us an eternal weight of glory beyond all comparison" (2 Cor. 4:17).

The sum of the matter is this: "God . . . has blessed us in Christ with every spiritual blessing"; we "have come to fulness of life in him" (Eph. 1:3; Col. 2:10). We do not have to do anything to achieve this new status, for it has been given to us in Christ. Nor can we add anything to the work which Christ has done on our behalf. Therefore, every teaching which suggests that we can move on to greater blessings than those which we have received through our initial faith in Christ is, in some way or other, actually adding some human work to the work of Christ and, consequently, dis-

ACTIVE OBEDIENCE

FOUR

We have shown how strenuously the Bible opposes the idea that Christian growth comes from something —anything—beyond Christ's work. The Bible teaches clearly that we are accepted by God only on the basis of Christ's death and resurrection on our behalf. Further, this "special-experience" approach to sanctification does not lead a person to be renewed in God's likeness. Instead, it produces either pride or despondency.

Having made clear the importance of Jesus' work for us, we come now to another basic aspect concerning growth in the Christian life, namely, the principle of active obedience. The relation of this to our central theme of humanness will be apparent. Jesus said, "Blessed are those who *hunger* and *thirst* for righteousness" (Mt. 5:6); and Paul says, "Let us not grow weary in well-doing" (Gal. 6:9).

Yet despite such plain statements of Scripture on this subject, one sometimes finds little teaching on active obedience. In fact, not a few consider it unspiritual to emphasize it.

Many say that we are simply to present ourselves to the Spirit, to open ourselves up to him and not make any effort to change; then the new life of the Spirit will flow out. Some say that this happens only after particular experiences—an experience of fullness, a second blessing, speaking in tongues as an evidence of Spirit baptism, or the breaking of the self to release the Spirit. After such an experience, it is said, the self is dead, the Spirit is released and there is no need or place for action.

This kind of teaching seeks to emphasize the uselessness of trying to practice righteousness ourselves, the uselessness of trying to imitate the Spirit's life. We are commanded to enter our rest and leave all new life to the Spirit. Activity must cease. The problem, we are told, is that we are still trying. A letter that was sent to us not long ago expressed this idea well: "Everytime you try to be good it's like saying to Jesus . . . I don't believe you. I can do better myself. . . . Everytime you try to be good it's a sin." This is an extreme example, but much teaching on the Christian life makes a similar mistake. This is an important issue and needs careful examination.

First, there is a legitimate use of the idea of *rest*. We rest thankfully on the finished work of Christ, knowing that we need add nothing to his work nor could we add anything to make ourselves more acceptable to God. Set free from sin, its guilt and the condemnation due to us, we are ransomed children, not indentured servants who must pay off a debt. We need not try to prove our worth to God. He accepts us as we are with all our sin and weakness because all is covered by Christ's righteousness and death.

Also, because our self-worth is measured not by how good we have been, but by the value God places on us, we need not prove anything to ourselves. He created us in his likeness and we therefore have dignity and value. Moreover, God has shown his love for us by giving his own Son to die for us. Confident in this, we do not strive by righteous acts to demonstrate our worth to God or to ourselves. In this sense we rest. We simply reach out the hands of faith knowing that apart from Christ we would be lost.

Second, there is also a right use of what is called *yielding* or giving ourselves to God. Certainly we are to yield ourselves entirely to him (Rom. 6:13, 19); we are to pray that he will work his will in us. Christ is the bridegroom, we are his bride. As such we are to offer ourselves to him; we are to pray day by day and moment by moment for God to strengthen us with his Spirit and produce his fruit in us. Or, changing the metaphor, Jesus is the vine, we are the branches. Our life and strength for growth flow from him; it is not self-generated (Jn. 15:4-5). On the other hand, however, we must not stop with resting and yielding, for the whole Bible on every page commands us to obey God actively throughout our lives.

The Christian and God's Law
This raises the question of the place of God's law in the life of the Christian. Often the law is totally neglected in teaching on the Christian life. It is regarded as having value under the old dispensation, but not in the new. Now that we are living in the new dispensation of the Spirit, the law, it is said, has no bearing on us. It serves only to expose our sinfulness and need of Christ—an evangelistic role. Appeal is made to Paul's statements. For example: "You have died to the law through the body of Christ," and "We are discharged from the law, dead to that which held us captive, so that we serve not under the old written code but in the new life of the Spirit" (Rom. 7:4, 6). These verses are taken to mean that the law is of no concern to believers.[1]

Paul uses the term *law* in several different ways. Sometimes *law* is used not simply to refer to God's moral standards and commandments, but to the principle of self-justification. So Paul says, "You are not under law [the principle of self-justification] but under grace" and "you have died to the law [the principle of self-justification] through the body of Christ" (Rom. 6:14; 7:4).

In these verses Paul contrasts the principle of grace with the principle of law. On one hand is the principle of justification by grace through the work of Christ; we add nothing to that work, but simply stretch out our empty hands to receive God's free gift of salvation. On the other hand is the principle of justification "by works of the law," under which we try to justify ourselves by our own good works. In this sense of law, Paul says we are "dead to the law," no longer under the law. As believers in Christ, accepted by God under the principle of grace, the law can no longer condemn us. We have "died with Christ" and therefore have died to the law.

Paul also speaks of the law as the pedagogue, custodian or schoolmaster of the Old Testament believers. They were minors who looked to God's grace which was not yet fully revealed as Christ had not yet died. The law restrained, supervised them and directed them to Christ.[2] We are not under the law in this sense either.

When describing God's moral law, however, Paul uses the term in a positive sense. For example, Paul says: "What then shall we say? That the law is sin? By no means! Yet, if it had not been for the law, I should not have known sin" (Rom. 7:7). The law exposes sin. This is a positive characteristic of the law because sin is wrong—it is against God's character and therefore contrary to the way we were made to be.

Again, Paul says, "The law is holy, and the commandment is holy and just and good. Did that which is good, then, bring death to me? By no means! It was sin, working death in me through what is good" (Rom. 7:12-13). The law is wholly good, there is no fault in it.

Paul even says "the law is spiritual" (Rom. 7:14). Notice how Paul brings together the Spirit and the law. The law is spiritual because it describes the kind of life I should be living in the Spirit. The law describes a spiritual life, a life that is pleasing to the Spirit. Therefore, Paul goes on to say, "I *delight* in the law of God, in my inmost self " (7:22). Because it is in the Spirit's law, Paul, a Christian, can delight in it and say, "I of myself serve the law of God with my mind" (7:25).

In fact, Paul concludes that the purpose of Christ's work is that the "righteous requirements of the law might be fully met in us, who do not live according to our sinful nature but according to the Spirit" (8:4 NIV). Paul is not speaking about justification here. He is referring to how we as justified Christians are to live each day. We are to fulfill the law's righteous requirements. Paul continually puts the law and the Spirit together in this passage. He first contrasts the *Spirit* and the sinful nature (8:6), and then shows how the *law* and sinful nature are opposed (8:7). Paul thus links the Spirit and the law. As Christians, then, we are to submit to God's law because the law tells us what is pleasing to God, it tells us what the things of the Spirit are and it tells us what it means practically to walk in the Spirit.

Law, in this sense, means not only the Ten Commandments, but the whole of God's moral law in the Old and New Testaments. The law includes all the moral commandments in the Sermon on the Mount, the rest of the Gospels and the New Testament letters. The law tells us what things in our behavior, either external or internal, are sinful. The law teaches us positively what we should do.

Clearly, the law and obedience to it play a very important part in our lives as Christians. What then is the relationship between the Spirit's work in us and our active obedience of the law?

In Romans, Paul speaks not only of yielding ourselves to God and reckoning ourselves dead to sin and alive to righteousness, but also he commands us to be active. For example, we are to "walk not according to the flesh [the sinful nature] but according to the Spirit" (8:4); and to "set [our] minds on the things of the Spirit" (8:5). By the Spirit we are to "put to death the deeds of the body [sinful nature]" (8:13).

The verbs Paul uses demand effort or action: "walk," "set the mind on," "put to death." He says that we are to live actively day by day according to the Spirit's desire, to be preoccupied with the things of the Spirit, to put sinful desires to death by the Spirit.

What does he mean by these expressions? Are we simply to wait for the Spirit to start moving us to some action? Does the Spirit tell us internally what "his things" are? Must we *feel* him empowering us to "walk" or to "put to death"? Paul does not leave us wondering. Clearly the Spirit does work into our lives, does empower us, and does lead us, even though we may not feel him doing so.

We are not simply informed inwardly by the Spirit; rather, we are informed explicitly by the law. Therefore, to set our minds on the things of the Spirit means to make God's law the absorbing object of our thoughts. We do not have to wait for the Spirit to tell us what to do, for he has already told us in his law, in the Word which is the Spirit's sword (Eph. 6:17).

Two very similar passages underline this point. In Ephesians 5:18, Paul commands us to be filled with the Spirit, and then, in the rest of the Epistle, sets out a particular pattern of life:

> Be filled with the Spirit, addressing one another in psalms and hymns and spiritual songs, singing and making melody to the Lord with all your heart, always and for everything giving thanks in the name of our Lord Jesus Christ to God the Father. Be subject to one another out of reverence for Christ. (5:18-21)

In Colossians 3:16, he commands us to let the Word of Christ dwell in us and again, in the following verses, sets out precisely the same pattern of life:

> Let the word of Christ dwell in you richly, teach and admonish one another in all wisdom, and sing psalms and hymns and spiritual songs with thankfulness in your hearts to God. And whatever you do, in word or deed, do everything in the name of the Lord Jesus, giving thanks to God the Father through him. (3:16-17)

The major difference between these two nearly identical passages is that one begins with a command to be filled with the Spirit; the other, with a command to be indwelt with the Word. Paul does not separate the internal work of the Spirit from the application of our minds and actions to the Word the Spirit has written in the Scriptures. Nor should we. The Spirit and the law stand together. We meditate on God's law and struggle to obey it. At the same time, we pray for the Spirit to fill us and strengthen us to change. We should be aware of what the law demands, so that in each moment of our lives, as we are faced with difficult personal relationships or with the sinful attitudes of our minds and hearts, we know what it means to walk according to the law and to put to death those attitudes which are against the law. In making such an effort, we are not working to achieve God's approval. We make the effort because we already have God's love and approval. As we stressed in chapter three, the motivation for doing what is good is the love of God declared in Christ.

James has this same emphasis on the importance of the law. "He who looks into the perfect law, the law of liberty, and perseveres, being no hearer that forgets but a doer that acts, he shall be blessed in his doing" (Jas. 1:25). The law is the "perfect law," the "law of liberty," the "royal law" (2:8). What he means is that the law brings freedom and fulfillment to our lives as we endeavor not simply to hear it but to act on its commands. Our action in obeying the law brings blessing. This is parallel to Paul's statements in Romans 8 that to set the mind on the Spirit brings life and peace, and that we will live if, by the Spirit, we put to death the deeds of the sinful nature (8:6, 13).

Why is it that practicing God's law brings freedom, blessing, life and peace? As we stressed in chapter one, humans are made like God; and the law, which is holy and good, describes what our lives are to be like in order for us to reflect God's character. The law describes the way we are intended to live.

Therefore, for those who are justified by Christ's perfect obedience to the law and by his death, the law is no longer negative, showing only the impossibility of perfectly meeting its demands. Instead, the law is now positive in its calling. The law is not arbitrary, nor is its intention restrictive. Rather, the law shows us the structure within which we can live a free and blessed human life, avoiding the pitfalls of sin. So the person who is most disobedient to the law is not only condemned by the law but eventually is also the least fulfilled person. As believers in Christ, we need no longer fear the law's penalties. Instead, we are set free to pursue with thankful hearts the course of life and peace set out in the law.

The Struggle

Still, the Spirit does not obey the law for us. Effort is necessary. The New Testament stresses that there is to be a struggle in the Christian life, a battle for obedience that requires all the energy of our wills. This struggle is due to the opposition in us between the sinful nature and the Spirit, between our bent to sin and our new desire to do right. It is *not* a sign of immaturity. Without this internal struggle and opposition there would be no evidence of new life. If we think that we have reached a plateau of rest beyond struggle and internal contradictions, then we are probably in a very dangerous state of self-deception.

This is why the New Testament compares the Christian life to the activity of the athlete, the wrestler and the soldier. From his own experience, Paul says, "Straining forward to what lies ahead, I press on toward the goal for the prize of the upward call of God in Christ Jesus" (Phil. 3:13-14). The author of Hebrews exhorts:

> Let us also lay aside every weight, and sin which clings so closely, and let us run with perseverence the race that is set before us. . . . In your struggle against sin you have not yet resisted to the point of shedding your blood. . . . Lift your drooping hands and strengthen your weak knees. . . . Strive for peace with all men, and for the holiness without which no one will see the Lord." (Heb. 12:1, 4, 12, 14)

Despite the New Testament's common depiction of the Christian life as struggle, strife and warfare, some teach that the normal Christian experience is rest and that struggle is abnormal. This is clearly contrary to Scripture.

In Colossians 3, Paul deals with two operations of this Christian warfare. The first is that of putting to death the old man; the second, putting on the new.

Put the Old Man to Death

The framework, once again, within which this warfare is waged is the finished work of Christ. We rest in him, knowing that our names are written in heaven. So, peace with God does not result from our own activity, nor is the Christian life lived simply in our own strength. When we strive to obey, we do so constantly thankful for the promise that the Holy Spirit will empower us.

So long as we keep our confidence in Christ in this way, struggling to obey brings freedom. Struggling to obey brings bondage only if the work of Christ, the basis for our acceptance and the source of our new life, is forgotten. Delivered from our guilt by Christ and dependent on his Spirit, we strive to supplement our faith with obedience, knowing this obedience will bring freedom. This, then, is the context of Paul's command:

> Put to death, therefore, whatever belongs to your earthly nature: sexual immorality, impurity, lust, evil desires and greed, which is idolatry. . . . You must rid yourselves of all such things as these: anger, rage, malice, slander, filthy language. (Col. 3:5, 8 NIV)

The Christian life is active, not passive. In fact, Paul's use of the aorist tense indicates that the activity of putting to death and putting off must be done moment by moment. It is something which is to go on all the time whenever we have sinful thoughts and desires. We are to kill or strangle the evil desires before they can grip our minds and actions. Using another figure, Paul says we are to discard temptations and destructive ideas like old clothes, continually peeling them off.

It is the continual destroying and discarding of sin which

brings conflict into our daily lives. Wrestling with temptation to anger, impurity, malice, slander and other sins is *normal* for the Christian because we still have a sinful nature and because Satan tries to make us disobey. Indeed, with the new life we have in the Spirit, these experiences of wrestling with sin are likely to become even more intense. They will not disappear until the day we die or until Christ returns, whichever comes first.

But we should realize that when the New Testament calls us to struggle against sin, the aim in view is wholly positive. To what man or woman does immorality, covetousness, anger, malice or slander bring any real and lasting peace or happiness? As we obey God in striving to put to death these and other sins, we should remember that all sin works destruction, and victory over sin brings blessing and peace.

Consider malice and bitterness, for example, against which Paul commands us to battle. If we indulge in bitter thoughts toward others or if we bear malice in our hearts, we bring unhappiness into our relationships with those around us; we also grieve the Holy Spirit, and we ourselves will be eaten up with passions far more deadly than cancer. Writing to Titus, Paul contrasts two ways of life:

> Remind them ... to speak evil of no one, to avoid quarreling, to be gentle, and to show perfect courtesy toward all men. For we ourselves were once foolish, disobedient, led astray, slaves to various passions and pleasures, passing our days in malice and envy, hated by men and hating one another. (Tit. 3:1-3)

Paul concludes that the one way of life is "excellent and profitable," while the other is "unprofitable and futile" (3:8-9).

All sin is to be put to death because it is destructive of what we were made to be. In that we have a sinful nature, sin is "natural" to us. But it is "unnatural" and abnormal in that we were made originally, and have been recreated by Christ, in the likeness of God himself. Therefore, these evil impulses are against our true (original and new) nature and must not be indulged internally or expressed externally, but rather confessed to God and put to death.

It follows, incidentally, that modern psychology is quite mistaken when it teaches that sinful attitudes must be expressed rather than curtailed and checked. We are told that suppression of our feelings leads to the inhibiting and crushing of ourselves and our freedom. But Paul says of expressing sinful feelings: "If you bite and devour one another take heed that you are not consumed by one another" (Gal. 5:15). They are not to be repressed (forced into the subconscious mind and ignored) but recognized for what they are—our own worst enemies—and then confessed as wrong and put away.

"But," someone may respond, "this all takes so much effort. I grow so weary of struggling against my sinful nature, and the devil too. Can't I just take it easy for a while?" It is because of this temptation to give up in the battle that the New Testament is full of commands to be vigilant and to continue to fight. So Paul says:

Now this I affirm and testify in the Lord, that you must no longer live as the Gentiles do . . . they have become callous and have given themselves up to licentiousness, greedy to practice every kind of uncleanness. You did not so learn Christ!—assuming that you have heard about him and were taught in him. (Eph. 4:17-21)

The battle against sin is obligatory for believers in Christ, especially in those areas of temptation which at times seem overwhelmingly difficult to handle. Satan finds such weak points in our armor and tries to sift us like wheat, weakening our resolve and undermining our sense of the wrongness of particular sins. At such times, and all believers experience them, we are not to give in without struggle. Rather, we are to put to death what is sinful.

We must not expect perfection, nor are we to despair because of our proneness to sin. John says, "If we say we have no sin, we deceive ourselves" (1 Jn. 1:8), and Paul admits: "Not that I have already obtained this or am already perfect" (Phil. 3:12). Hence, the question we are to ask ourselves is not "Have I achieved perfection?" or even "Am I gaining victory in any area?" but "Am I struggling against sin? Am I involved in the battle?"

Only as we strive to put to death the desires of our sinful natures do we become truly conscious of how great our gratitude for Christ's work should be and how dependent we are on the power of the Holy Spirit. In our weakness, wearied by the battle against sin, we learn to cry out, "Wretched man that I am! Who will deliver me from this body of death? Thanks be to God through Jesus Christ our Lord!" (Rom. 7:24-25). Some read Paul here as if he were suggesting passivity. Far from saying, "Give up trying," Paul is making the point that our very striving against sin causes us to be aware of the riches of Christ's work for us and our need for the Spirit's help. Only as we actively obey God's commands to put away sin and do right do we learn to appreciate truly the love of Christ and grow in our dependence on his Spirit.

Put on the New Man
The other side of the call to put sin to death is the command to put on the new man. It is very important to hold together these two aspects (negative and positive) of our active obedience. Why is this?

Some teaching on the Christian life stresses the necessity of dealing with sin before we can begin to live the new life of the Spirit. Instead of putting the negative ahead of the positive, Paul keeps both emphases together. For if we just deal with the negative, there is the danger of becoming frustrated, discouraged by our weakness and sinfulness or growing introspective about our failures.

Many are so caught up in their difficulties that they cannot begin to think about putting on the new man and caring for other people. This may be the root of the problem. Because we are not made to live inside ourselves, the more we do so, the more mixed up we become. Introspection breeds psychological problems. The only way out of this "ingrownness" is to recognize the worth we have in Christ and to struggle to practice the characteristics of the new man whether we feel like doing so or not. In fact, we can be quite sure that if we have been living inside ourselves, we will not feel like practicing compassion, gentleness or love. Emotion sometimes has to follow, rather than precede, action.

Putting on new patterns of life means, very simply, that we should begin to think about others.

> Put on then, as God's chosen ones, holy and beloved, compassion, kindness, lowliness, meekness, and patience, forbearing one another and, if one has a complaint against another, forgiving each other; as the Lord has forgiven you, so you also must forgive. And above all these put on love, which binds everything together in perfect harmony. (Col. 3:12-14)

It is only as we begin to think of others and not just about ourselves, that there is any possibility for change in our lives. We are not made to relate only inwardly to ourselves. God has made us in his image and we are to reflect the personal relationships which exist within the Trinity and to practice toward others the love, kindness and humility which God has expressed toward us. Therefore, as we begin to love others, to forgive, to forbear and be humble, we are fulfilling our nature as the image of God and we will consequently enjoy the fruits of such a life.

Christ, being the only one who has ever lived in perfect conformity to the likeness of God, has made it possible for us to put on the "new nature" and become new men and women. How has he done this?

Because of his life of obedience, including his death and resurrection, Jesus brought about something new—a different order of things—which will be consummated at the final victory when he returns. Because Christ's work affects not just humanity, but the whole creation, there will be a new heaven and a new earth (Rom. 8:19-21). There will be a new Jerusalem, each of us will have a new name and we shall all sing a new song. In fact, God says, "Behold, I make all things new" (Rev. 21:5). The goal of Christ's work is the new cretion, the regeneration of all things.

This newness, however, is not simply future, not only a glory ahead which encourages us to resist sin. The newness is a present reality. We are called to put on the new man now. One day even our bodies will be made new and will no longer be subject to sickness, corruption and death. But already, every believer in Christ is a new creation. We may not feel new, but already we have a new relationship with God through the Spirit who changes us day by day as he shows us the glories of Christ's redeeming work (2 Cor. 3:17-18).

The Spirit is called the earnest and the first fruits of the new age. His task is to produce in us now the first fruits of that future glory. As Christians it is our privilege and responsibility to be the new humanity, a new race separated from the society around us—separated by the quality of life we are living, not by removing ourselves. We are now to be God's first fruits of the new creation which will one day transform the world. "You are a chosen race, a royal priesthood, a holy nation, God's own people, that you may declare the wonderful deeds of him who called you out of darkness into his marvelous light" (1 Pet. 2:9).

We are to reckon by faith that we have newness of life in Christ. We also are called to bring this newness into realization in our lives day by day. It is in this sense that we are to "put on the new man."

One of the dominant schools of psychology has taught that we are completely determined by our genetic make-up or by our environment so that there is no possibility of newness in an individual's life. We are formed by the mold in which we were set by our genes, our parents and our education. Some will say, therefore, that it is impossible for any person to change. But this is not what the Scripture teaches.

We do not have to conform to our past; we do not have to be determined by our environment. There is the possibility of change, of transformation, of putting on the new man because, first, all people are made in God's image with significance and, second, because through faith in Christ and the indwelling of the Holy Spirit likeness to God is being renewed. We may come from terribly difficult backgrounds where years of mistreatment and emotional starvation have built up frustrations, fear of rejection, resentments and all sorts of problems, but the Scriptures and the Holy Spirit hold before us the possibility of change.

The people whom Paul evangelized and to whom he wrote came from difficult environments and had various psychological problems, but he called them, as he calls us, to declare God's mercies in a new life. No one need say, "There is no possibility of change for me; I am the one person whose problems are so acute that I am helplessly trapped by my past."

Compassion, Thankfulness and Obedience

As we pointed out earlier, the characteristics of the new nature center on our personal relationships with others. For each of these characteristics—lowliness, compassion, forgiveness, forbearance and love—Christ is the supreme example or pattern. We are to practice compassion as Jesus did; we are to be lowly in heart as Jesus was; we are to forgive as Jesus forgave; we are to be forbearing with the weaknesses and faults of others as Jesus was and is forbearing; we are to love as Jesus loved.

Instances of Jesus' compassion, for example, fill the gospel record. In compassion (the leper expected Jesus, like others, to shun him) Jesus reached out and touched a leper and healed him (Mk. 1:41-42). Often he was filled with pity for the sick and suffering and for those laboring under sin. God himself is the "Father of mercies and God of all comfort" (2 Cor. 1:3). Having been created in his likeness, we should follow his example in dealing with people (especially as revealed in Jesus Christ). This mercy is to be shown in practical ways: "If anyone has the world's goods and sees his brother in need, yet closes his heart against him, how does God's love abide in him?" (1 Jn. 3:17).

John's exhortation shows how thankfulness and obedience go hand in hand. We are called not simply to imitate Christ, but to remember his bearing toward us. As we do, our hard hearts are softened and we turn and try to love others. If it is difficult to forgive someone's fault or to put up with their weaknesses, then we must recall how much Christ has put up with in us and how much we have been forgiven and then forgiveness will be less difficult. Christ's love to us is the source and motivating power of our ability to forgive and forbear.

Furthermore, notice that the commands to forgive and to forbear (as well as many others) assume the sinfulness of others. We should expect each other to be sinful, unpleasant at times and difficult to live with. That is what it means to be a member of the human race at present. If we expect perfection from others or from ourselves, we will only succeed in being unable to appreciate anything that anyone does, or for that matter anything we do. To expect perfection from any but God is to crush them.

Now the New Testament certainly calls us to perfection (it would be absurd to call us to be half-loving or to be forgiving only half the time). But we must not interpret this call to perfection as a model which, if and when we fail to live up to it, makes us feel destroyed and useless. If we expect perfection (or anything like it) from ourselves or others, we are putting ourselves under the law again in a very negative and destructive way. The gospel says loud and clear that we are sinful and we will remain sinful until the day we die. We have been freed from the condemnation of imperfection by the work of Christ. Let us glory in that freedom and not, by setting up false expectations, put ourselves or anyone else under a yoke no one can bear.

Aware of our freedom from condemnation and filled with a sense of the love of Christ, we now can begin practically to see the needs of others and to care for them. As we begin to love others practically, our internal problems, which seemed insurmountable, will gradually begin to disappear. This may take years, but because we are humans made in

God's image and because to practice the kind of life that reflects his character is to fulfill our own nature, we will surely be blessed and will experience life in a richer way. Let us be obedient to our calling and enjoy the fruits of humanness.

THE HOLY SPIRIT AND THE SELF: SOVEREIGNTY AND RESPONSIBILITY

FIVE

"Faith a gift?

The work of the Holy Spirit in the life of the believer is a clear emphasis throughout the New Testament. The Holy Spirit plays a very important part both in a person's coming to faith and growth to maturity. In fact, without the work of the Spirit there can be no faith nor any growth into conformity with Christ. Thus the Spirit is sovereign in the Christian's life.

Is the principle of humanness overruled, then, because of the necessity of the Spirit's work? No.

The sovereignty of the Spirit and the principle of humanness are affirmed side by side in the New Testament. Indeed, far from nullifying it, the sure knowledge that the Spirit will work in me to change me and strengthen me *establishes* the *necessity* of my working out my own salvation. Rather than discouraging me, making me feel that I can only wait helplessly for the Spirit to work, the knowledge that the Spirit is the sovereign Lord over my life is a source of comfort and encouragement.

In this chapter we will consider first who the Spirit is, then discuss his work—regeneration (the beginning of the Christian life) and sanctification (growth in the Christian life).

The Personal Spirit

Who or what is the Holy Spirit? Many people are confused by this question. The Jehovah's Witnesses, for example, deny that the Holy Spirit is either personal or that he is God. They speak of him as a kind of effluence or power coming out from God the Father. Unhappily, Christians sometimes speak in the same way. This has on the surface some justification as the New Testament does speak of being "filled" with the Spirit, of the Holy Spirit being "poured out" and being "made to drink" of the Spirit (see, for example, Acts 2:4, 17; 1 Cor. 12:13). The New Testament or indeed the whole Bible as a unit, however, speaks unmistakably of the Holy Spirit as both fully God and a person.

The Spirit is the creator of the world (Gen. 1:2; Job 26:13), the creator of man (Job 33:4) and the author of the Scriptures (2 Pet. 1:21; Heb. 3:7). That creation and inspiration are clearly ascribed elsewhere in Scripture to God himself makes it plain that the Spirit is God. Examples of other characteristics and tasks of the eternal God applied to the Holy Spirit include the omnipresence of the Spirit—we cannot escape his presence (Ps. 139); he knows the secrets of our hearts and the thoughts of God (1 Cor. 2:10-13); the indwelling Spirit makes the believer the temple of God (1 Cor. 3:16) and the temple of the Holy Spirit (1 Cor. 6:19). The Spirit is fully God.

Anyone who denies that the Spirit is God can do so only by ignoring the majority of the biblical passages which speak of the Spirit. By dwelling on a few passages which state that the Spirit proceeds from the Father they draw the unwarranted conclusion that he is less than the Father. At the root of this position is the conviction that God must be absolute unity—that there can be only one person in the Godhead. But the glory of the biblical position is that God is and always has been three persons. Thus God is truly personal: the attributes of personality (for example, love and communication, Jn. 17:24) are fulfilled within the Godhead.

The deity of the Spirit and the deity of Christ should never be treated as if they were secondary and embarrassing, though necessary, doctrines. We should glory that God is three persons—Father, Son and Spirit—each fully God and yet each a distinct person. Because this is true, we can be sure that we live in a universe where personality has ultimate value.

Christians often betray their unfamiliarity with this aspect of biblical teaching by speaking of the Spirit as "it" or in very vague terms, as if the Spirit were like an electrical charge or force. The apparently impersonal, even inanimate terminology of Scripture ("filling," "pouring out") does not point to the impersonality of the Spirit, however, but to the intimacy of the believer's personal relationship with him.

The Spirit is the Paraclete, the one called alongside each Christian just as Jesus was alongside his disciples as their counselor, guide, teacher, friend, comforter and advocate in their defense (Jn. 14:16). Each believer has as close a relationship with the Spirit as the disciples had with Christ. The only difference is that the Spirit is not present in bodily form as Jesus was, and thus we cannot see, touch or hear him as the disciples saw, touched and heard Jesus. From our side the Spirit's work is secret just as the blowing of the wind is secret (Jn. 3:8). But he is not less real because of that, nor is his work within us and alongside us any less personal.

Elsewhere in the New Testament we see an equal emphasis on the personness of the Spirit. He wills (1 Cor. 12:11), prays for us and has a mind (Rom. 8:27), can be lied to (Acts 5:3) and can be grieved (Eph. 4:30). All these are experiences of a person, not a force.

The Sovereign Spirit
Because the Spirit is God it also follows that he is sovereign

over all of reality. Therefore, the Bible speaks of the Spirit's lordship over the believer's life.

In John 3, Jesus says that a person must be born of the Spirit in order to enter the kingdom of God. Paul says that the faith of the Corinthian Christians is evidence that the Spirit of the living God has worked in their hearts (2 Cor. 3:3). While dead in transgressions and sins, we are given life by the Spirit (Eph. 2:1; 2 Cor. 3:6). Further, Paul says that no one can say Jesus is Lord except by the Spirit (1 Cor. 12:3), and reminds Titus that we are saved not by righteous things we have done but by the washing of rebirth and renewal in the Holy Spirit (Tit. 3:5).

These and many other passages indicate the necessity of the Spirit's sovereign work in salvation. He is the one who takes the initiative, just as parents take the initiative in begetting and conceiving a child. That is why Jesus uses the language of birth in telling Nicodemus how he may enter the kingdom (Jn. 3:3-8).

Although his initiative is essential for salvation, the Spirit, nevertheless, does not override or violate our personality. Nor does his sovereignty cancel the principle of humanness. We are not totally passive in relationship to God. At this point the analogy of the parents begetting the child breaks down, for the child has no say as to whether he or she is to be born. It is not the same for us. But, sadly, some have taught that because we are dead in sin and need the life-giving work of the Spirit, we therefore cannot seek for God and put our trust in him. They have said it is useless to encourage others to consider the evidence for Christianity in order to persuade them of the truth of the gospel.

It should be clear from our discussion, however, that the sovereignty of God does not crush human activity. The work of the Spirit does not mean we are passive—machines operated by remote control or sticks and stones to be dragged into the kingdom.

In fact, it is the sovereignty of God which establishes the principle of humanness. Human creatures, like the Creator

THINK=DECIDE=ACT

whose image they bear, think, decide and act. Our actions and decisions are not sovereign over all reality as God's are, because we are finite and limited, but they are nevertheless significant. Remember that the Spirit of God is personal; he works alongside and in us, rather than controlling us as if we were not personal.

The New Testament writers clearly did not shrink from placing human responsibility side by side with the sovereignty of the Spirit in bringing us to new life. Jesus juxtaposes these two in a remarkable way: "No one knows the Father except the Son and those to whom the Son chooses to reveal him. Come to me, all you who are weary and burdened, and I will give you rest" (Mt. 11:27-28 NIV). Here is a very strong statement of sovereignty followed by an urgent plea by the second person of the Trinity that anyone who feels weary and burdened should come to him for rest. In John 6, the two ideas occur side by side again. On the one hand there is the necessity of the drawing work of the Father (6:44) and on the other, the call to believe in Jesus—to eat his flesh and drink his blood (6:54), and to look to the Son and believe in him (6:40). The individual is to be active in looking and believing.

Paul's own life illustrates how these two things are held together. As we have seen already, he speaks of new life coming from the Spirit. And yet, because he knows that this does not override human responsibility, Paul is aware that the way he behaves will affect people's response to the truth (1 Cor. 9:19), he spends months trying to persuade people of the truth of Christianity (Acts 19:8; 18:4; 17:2), and he commands his listeners to repent. This is the pattern throughout the New Testament and the conclusion is clear: humans have the responsibility to repent and believe because they are significant.

This same significance enables them also to resist the Holy Spirit. To those who were about to kill him, Stephen said, "You stiff-necked people, uncircumcised in heart and ears, you always resist the Holy Spirit. As your fathers did, so do you" (Acts 7:51). Jesus himself says much the same: "O Jerusalem, Jerusalem, killing the prophets and stoning those who are sent to you! How often would I have gathered your children together as a hen gathers her brood under her wings, and you would not!" (Mt. 23:37).

Who Can Resist God?

Some may ask at this point, How can you say that God is sovereign and also that man is so significant that he can resist God? Are you not making an irrational statement? Surely such an assertion is contrary to the laws of logic.

When considering what is rational or irrational, there are several questions to be answered. We take up these questions in chapter seven. For now, it will suffice to say that, in order to be reasonable, a statement must conform to the two sources of knowledge we have—our experience of the nature of reality, and most importantly the information God has given us in the Bible. We might also ask, What are the alternatives to the proposed statement or view, and do these alternatives conform to the data we have from the Bible and from experience?

The first alternative to the position we have presented would say that God is sovereign and that therefore man is not ultimately significant. The biblical statements about predestination, about God's initiative in salvation, are taken to mean that choice is only an illusion. Judas, for example, had no choice but to betray Christ; Joseph's brothers made no real choice when they sold him into slavery; we make no choices either to become Christians or to grow as Christians. There is no choice, only the secret will of God being worked out on the stage of history.

This alternative leaves us no options. If God is sovereign, we cannot be responsible. There is no halfway ground.

This categorical rejection of human responsibility creates several problems. Most importantly, much teaching of Scripture has to be ignored in order to deny human responsibility in the sense of determining one's own life. This distorts scriptural data by conforming it to a preconceived idea: if Scripture says God is foreordaining things, this logically means people cannot have choice. But the Scripture concedes no such dilemma. It consistently affirms both God's sovereignty and human responsibility. It will not do to say that God's plan is only his foreknowledge, in order to "make room" for human choice. We are not justified in saying that foreordaining means only that God knows what humans and devils will decide ahead of time. This implies that God merely confirms the choices of others, rather than acting to work out his own purposes. But Jesus says that every hair of our heads is numbered, meaning not that God knows how many hairs there are on our heads, but that nothing happens to us apart from the Father's will (Mt. 10:29-30). And Peter says that Jesus was delivered up to be crucified "according to the definite plan and foreknowledge of God" (Acts 2:23). God has made plans and is working them out in history. Humans too make choices: "Why will you die, O house of Israel? For I have no pleasure in the death of anyone, says the Lord GOD; so turn, and live" (Ezek. 18:31-32). The alternative of accepting *only* God's sovereignty fails the first test—it is unbiblical.

This alternative also fails when measured against our experience of life. We continually experience ourselves making choices and we see results of those choices—often to our shame. Yet, when we pray in faith, we are convinced that God is able to hear our prayers and act into this world. All prayer is meaningless if God is not able to work out his sovereign will.

At the same time, unless we are convinced of the value of our own actions, we will never pray. If nothing we do could possibly affect God, it would be pointless to pray. Thus, the believer's experience of reality in praying and seeing prayers answered establishes both God's sovereignty and human significance, and thereby makes irrational and untrue the assertion that, in order to uphold the power of God, we must deny human choice.

The second alternative is equally irrational. To say that

because man's choice is real, God cannot be preordaining at the same time, is subject to the same criticism as the first alternative. Scripture does indeed teach that we have choice, but one cannot draw the conclusion, as some have done, that if man is free to choose then his actions are of necessity unpredictable.[1] Such a view removes God from the throne on which Scripture places him.

We must work with *all* the data of Scripture and of our experience, and not consider one aspect of Scripture's teaching as a grid through which all else must be put. The expositor, for example, who looks at a statement like, "Have I any pleasure in the death of the wicked, says the Lord GOD, and not rather that he should turn from his way and live?" (Ezek. 18:23) and insists that it must refer to the elect only, rather than to humankind in general, is guilty of such a rationalization. From a proof text the expositor has erected a system. All statements of Scripture which question this system are ignored. The same is true of the person who says that God only *reacts* to our choices, rather than *acting* to establish his own choices.

Someone may still respond, "I think it is against reason to hold to sovereignty and responsibility at the same time." But if no problem with holding both is indicated by the data we have from Scripture and experience, then it is irrational to reject either. If we have not considered such a possibility before, then we have to enlarge our view of reality rather like the physicist who discovers evidence which suggests that light is made up of particles as well as waves, or the child who realizes that the world is bigger than his own village.

Still, we must say that we do not see *how* the two work together. We do not understand how in practice God can be Lord of the universe, acting out his purposes, and that we also—made in his image—make our own significant choices and actions which even God respects. Yet the Scripture teaches this, our experience confirms it, and it is the conviction behind our every prayer.

We often do not understand the *how* of reality. We do not understand, for example, how Jesus was both God and man or how this worked out internally for him. Yet all Christians have affirmed with the apostles that Jesus was both God and man. We know too that our salvation requires him to be both God and man—God, in order to be a sufficient offering for the sins of all and to have power over death, and man, to be our representative who could offer himself in our place. We do not understand how, through the physical process of reproduction, a person can be born who is human—who loves, is moral, is significant, and who since Adam has a sinful nature. Nor do we understand how God created the universe simply by speaking.

We understand *that* these things are true, we can support them by data from Scripture and experience, and we can see why alternative positions are false. But often, simply because we are finite (see chapter eight), our understanding of how things work is limited.

The Spirit and Sanctification

We turn now to the scriptural teaching about sovereignty and responsibility in sanctification. The Spirit is sovereign over Christian growth. Both Peter and Paul speak of the sanctifying work of the Spirit (1 Pet. 1:2; 2 Thess. 2:13). The Spirit is the one who sanctifies us, who causes us to become righteous in our behavior. It is the Spirit who cries, "Abba! Father!" in our hearts (Gal. 4:6). Paul speaks of our love in the Spirit (Col. 1:8), joy given by the Spirit (1 Thess. 1:6), the unity of the Spirit (Eph. 4:3) and the fruit of the Spirit (Gal. 5:22).

In this last passage Paul makes it abundantly clear that it is the Spirit's work to produce in us the fruit of love, joy, peace, patience, kindness, goodness, faithfulness, gentleness and self-control. Because we have an anointing from the Holy One we all know the truth (1 Jn. 2:20). We know that God lives in us by the Spirit he has given us (1 Jn. 3:24; 4:13). All of these passages stress the necessity of the Spirit's work in sanctification. The texts referred to (and many others) deal with every aspect of the Christian life and therefore demonstrate that the Holy Spirit is, and must be, active in order for there to be any growth in the individual Christian or in a body of Christians together.

Because of the supposed antithesis between God's sovereignty and human responsibility, some have taught that the Christian must be passive in sanctification. But if one stresses the necessity of the Spirit's internal work in the believer without a corresponding emphasis on the equally important biblical teaching on the responsibility of the individual, the result can be the stunting of growth.

This stunting may take one of several forms. For example, a person may insist that because the Spirit is sovereign he is free to do what he likes, saying, "It doesn't matter what I do; I know that I am elect." The outcome is a dangerous complacency accompanied by disregard for God's holiness. The writer of Hebrews addresses such a person again and again: "Strive for peace with all men, and for the holiness without which no one will see the Lord" (Heb. 12:14; see also 10:26-27; 12:25-29).

Another person, taught that the Spirit will do everything to sanctify her, may begin to wonder at the lack of change in her life. Having built up a series of expectations as to what the Spirit will do in her, she may even begin to blame God because these expectations have not been met. "I have the right to joy and peace, for they are the Spirit's fruit, his responsibility, not mine. But where are they?" The result is often a cynical mocking at the precious truths of the gospel because of unbalanced teaching. (See the warning of Hebrews 12:15 about a "root of bitterness" springing up and defiling a believer.)

A third possible result of a lack of emphasis on the believer's role may be unhealthy introspection. He begins to ask himself, "Am I elect?" "Is the Spirit crying, 'Daddy! Father!' in my heart?" "Am I being sanctified by the Spirit?" "Do I have the joy of the Spirit?" Believers must indeed ask themselves whether they are in the faith, and self-examination to expose sin is important. But introspective questions and continual searchings within for signs of the Spirit's presence and work will only have the effect of undermining confidence in salvation.

We have known of some who did not feel they could take the Lord's Supper for many years after becoming believers because a one-sided emphasis on sovereignty rendered them unable to rest confidently on Christ's work. They felt they could not see the internal marks of an elect person which they had been told to expect. This is very sad as confidence in one's salvation is essential for growth in the Christian life.

The fact that this is often the result of unbalanced teaching should cause us to treasure a proper biblical balance. While stressing the sovereign power of the sanctifying Spirit, God also teaches us in his Word of the necessity of human activity in sanctification. This is the truth which sets us free.

Earlier we looked at a text which shows how we are saved through the renewing work of the Spirit (Tit. 3:5-6). Strikingly, Paul uses this very teaching as the basis for emphasizing the believer's responsibility to act. He says, "I want you to stress these things [that salvation is God's work], so that those who have trusted in God may be careful to devote themselves to doing what is good" (3:8 NIV). Paul appeals to the Spirit's sovereignty not to discourage human action, but to *insist* on it.

The same point is made even more strongly in Philippians 2:12: "Continue to work out your salvation with fear and trembling, for it is God who works in you to will and do what pleases him" (NIV). Here again we find a startling juxtaposition. For the Christian who is uneasy with the idea of stressing both the sovereignty of God and the responsibility of the individual believer there can be no more perplexing text. The reason given for my unceasing and very careful activity is God's unceasing action in me through his Spirit. It is particularly remarkable that the Philippians were encouraged to "work out your own *salvation*." Paul underlines, as it were, the absolutely necessary involvement of the human will in salvation alongside the intention and will of God.

And this is not surprising given the Bible's teaching on who God is and what it means to be human. God is not an inscrutable force like Allah handing out immutable decrees with no recognition of the persons he has made. He does not simply knock people at random off the rope bridge of life into the abyss below regardless of their cries for mercy. Rather, the God of the Bible is truly personal; he loves and cherishes the persons he has made in his own image. He is sovereign and yet he also recognizes that our nature, as persons made like him, is to will, decide and act. Any attempt to deny one side or the other is simply a rationalization.

We have seen how in his first letter John teaches the lordship of the Spirit in the Christian's life, while also emphasizing human action. In 1 John 3:24 he tells us that we know Christ lives in us and we in him by the Spirit he has given us. However, John does not leave us wondering how to tell whether or not the Spirit *is* in us. This could begin a process of inward questioning: "Do I *feel* the Spirit living in me?" "Am I feeling so weak and sinful and empty because the Spirit is not really in me?" Being a good pastor, John gives us a clear test. But this test is obscured by the chapter division. As it stands chapter 3 ends with the statement, "We know that he abides in us, by the Spirit which he has given us."

But when we ignore the chapter division and look at the first verses of chapter 4, we find the command: "Do not believe every spirit, but test the spirits to see whether they are from God." Then John continues, "This is how you can recognize the Spirit of God: Every spirit that acknowledges that Jesus Christ has come in the flesh is from God" (NIV).

Notice that his test for recognition of the Spirit's presence is a doctrinal one—does the person (whether myself or someone else) acknowledge that Jesus Christ has come in the flesh? If the answer is "yes," then the teaching or the person is from God and has his Spirit. Conversely, anyone who denies Jesus does not have the Spirit of God.

John reinforces this in the next verses. He speaks of the greatness of the Spirit who is in us and through whom we have victory (v. 4)—emphasizing that the Spirit's lordship is the basis for our confidence and security. But again he provides a test for how we can know whether we are from God and whether we have this great One dwelling in us. "Whoever knows God listens to us" (v. 6). The test of whether God's Spirit is living and working in us is whether we listen to the apostles' teaching or disregard it. If we listen, then we know we have the Spirit of truth.

Even as John speaks of the Spirit's work, he emphasizes that we are responsible. Throughout John's letter he insists that we are born of God, that we are anointed by the Holy One, that God lives in us, that God first loved us. And it is just because God himself has worked in us that we are to be obedient to God's commands to love one another, care for one another's practical needs, and hold fast to the truth.

Without this understanding of the relationship between the Spirit's work and our work, there will be no growth. If we are not sure that the Spirit is our sovereign Lord who works to restore us, then we will be overcome by our own weakness and sinfulness. We may struggle on valiantly for a time but if we realize how sinful we really are, the strain of sanctifying ourselves unaided will gradually wear us down. We will feel discouragement and helplessness when faced with the seemingly insatiable demands of God's Word.

If on the other hand we are not convinced that we have a part to play in our own growth, that there is something we can do about our weakness and our sinful attitudes, then we will hold God responsible for our failures and will begin to resent our uselessness. As someone once said to us, "I have a right to expect joy and peace in my life—these are the Spirit's fruit, not mine—but where are they?" It was a cry of anger against God—anger at what this person felt was the Spirit's failure to fulfill his responsibility toward him.

To both these misrepresentations the Scripture speaks loudly and clearly. The basis of our action in struggling with weakness or sin is the confidence that God's Spirit works in us, that we are not alone, that he will work in us to change us. Also, he calls us to action: "Make every effort to add to your faith goodness; and to goodness, knowledge; and to knowledge, self-control; and to self-control, perseverance; and to perseverance, godliness; and to godliness, brotherly kindness; and to brotherly kindness, love" (2 Pet. 1:5-7 NIV). Or as Paul says, "I labor, struggling with all the energy he so powerfully works in me" (Col. 1:29 NIV).

So we too strive, knowing the Spirit strives in us. For example, we labor at proclaiming the good news of the gospel, trying hard to convince people of the truth, earnestly encouraging them to turn to Christ in faith, pointing as carefully as we can to the evidence for the Christian position. And we labor with the confidence that the Spirit is working alongside us, within us in our lives, through our words and in the hearts of the hearers. As Peter says, "We are witnesses . . . and so is the Holy Spirit" (Acts 5:32). As in evangelism, so in every aspect of our Christian lives we are to work hard day after day, praying that God out of his glorious riches may strengthen us with power through his Spirit in our inner being (Eph. 3:16 NIV).

This balance of the Scripture is to be found in every area where both God and people are involved. Living the Christian life is analogous with the writing of the Scriptures. Though penned by human authors and bearing the mark of their personalities, the Bible is authored by God and is therefore free of mistakes in whatever it says, whether in the area of theology, morals, history or science. Even in giving us his infallible Word, the Spirit did not override the significance of those who wrote the various books. Nor does he do so now as he works in us who believe and who press on toward the goal to win the prize for which God has called us heavenward in Christ Jesus.

AFFIRMING THE SELF AND DENYING THE SELF

SIX

While discussing the organizing principle in chapter one, we mentioned that sanctification must not be viewed as a negative experience for the believer but essentially as a positive one. For this reason we described the Bible's view of spiritual experience as an affirmation of life, that is, as a recovery of the human experience lost at the Fall.

Some passages in the Bible which deal with the Christian's experience, however, seem hard to understand. For example, Jesus told his disciples they must lose their lives (Mk. 8:35). Paul said that the believer has died with Christ and must "seek the things that are above" (Col. 3:1).

There are a number of passages like these which seem to give a negative view of the Christian's experience. Do they contradict our theme of affirmation? Is it right, for example, to describe Jesus' statements about losing one's life and denying oneself as affirmations of life? What of his commands that we must hate our own lives (Lk. 14:26; Jn. 12:25)? Is his command to the rich ruler—"Sell all that you have"—

a principle for all Christians? And does it exclude the possibility of having possessions and enjoying them (Lk. 18:22)?

Because asceticism is such a common problem in the
church and because these passages appear to encourage asceticism, it is very important to look carefully at them. As
was said in chapter two, asceticism raises its head in some
form or other every generation. People think that being a
Christian—being spiritual—means giving up everything
that is enjoyable and crushing whatever inner impulses
they have simply because they are part of human experience. This attitude is not confined to Christendom, of course.
Throughout history there has been a tendency toward asceticism within the religions of the world, so that for ordinary
men and women "religion" has become synonymous with the
negative, the drab, the gaunt, the unnatural. The monk, for
example, gives up everything, renounces his possessions,
lives in great austerity, shaves his head and is celibate. This
is the ideal of "being spiritual." The "religious," as they are
called, even seem like athletes in a race of negation—each
trying to outdo the other in severity toward the body by sit-
ting on beds of nails or in ice-bound caves, never speaking
and eating hardly anything.

Those who are "too weak" for this asceticism imagine,
therefore, that religion is against the experiences which
make up their ordinary life—the enjoyment of food and
drink, of husband or wife, of leisure and creativity. Religion
appears to them to be a monster that eats up the self.

The problem, however, is that some Christians have argued that asceticism is right and moreover have sought to
justify this attitude by means of the passages we want to
look at now. Our choice of passages is not complete, yet is
sufficient to indicate how the apparent difficulties of interpretation are resolved. In the context of the Bible as a whole
even those passages which appear to contradict the organizing principle are found to uphold it. For convenience we
have divided them into three sections—affirming the self,
not the sinfulness of self; affirming the self and suffering

with Christ; and affirming the self and redeeming the world.

Affirming the Self, Not the Sinfulness of Self

This category needs little explanation for the distinction between the self and sin has been dealt with already (pp. 36-37, 46, 51-52). The Bible is never opposed to human experience as such; to experience life includes touch and taste, work and play, love and beauty. What it does oppose is human experience which is sinful.

A good example of this category of passages is the statement by John. "Do not love the world or the things in the world. If any one loves the world, love for the Father is not in him" (1 Jn. 2:15). This seems at first sight to be advocating asceticism. It seems to reject all those things we enjoy in life which are associated with the physical. And some Christians have read it like this. "The world" has been taken to mean everything having to do with our physical experience, especially the things that give us pleasure. 1 John 2:15 has become a proof text for those who wish to confine spiritual experience within very narrow bounds of religious do's and secular don'ts.

But such a reading of the passage is quite wrong for John goes on in the immediate context to clarify what he means by "loving the world." He says, "For all that is in the world, [that is,] the lust of the flesh and the lust of the eyes and the pride of life, is not of the Father but is of the world" (2:16). These are the things we are not to love. John is not excluding the enjoyment of God's creation and all its beauty, nor even the enjoyment of man's creation—music or painting—nor even the enjoyment of physical experiences in general, such as eating and drinking. He is simply excluding a wrong attitude which does not honor God and which fails to see that God is the ultimate origin of everything, the one who gives significance to all of life. Such experiences are wrong, not because they have taken place literally "in the world," in the sphere of physical reality, but because of lust and pride.

The same is true of Paul's negative statements concerning

"the body," "the flesh" and "the world." He says, for example, "If you live according to the flesh you will die, but if by the Spirit you put to death the deeds of the body you will live" (Rom. 8:13). Elsewhere in his writings, Paul makes it obvious that by these expressions (*flesh* and *body*) he is not being negative toward human experience.

Paul explains *flesh* in Galatians 5:19-21, for example, where he lists the kinds of experience which are included within the scope of this term. "Do not gratify the desires of the flesh.... Now the works of the flesh are plain: fornication, impurity, licentiousness, idolatry, sorcery, enmity, strife, jealousy, anger, selfishness, dissension, party spirit, envy, drunkenness, carousing, and the like." In verse 26 he adds, "Let us have no self-conceit, no provoking of one another, no envy of one another."

Clearly, "the deeds of the body" (Rom. 8:13) are not physical deeds as such but sinful actions and thoughts. It is these that have to be put away by the Christian. And this is just what one would expect from the apostle who wrote, "Everything created by God is good, and nothing is to be rejected if it is received with thanksgiving" (1 Tim. 4:4).

The distinction between self and sin is further illuminated by looking at the Bible's attitude toward possessions. There is a great deal of confusion about this subject today, due in part to pressure from socialist and Marxist thought and in part to a reaction to the ugliness of materialism in the West, a reaction, let us quickly say, which is fully justified. Christian tradition has always included the ascetic ideal, however, and some Christians have felt guilty, thinking that to possess something, and in particular to enjoy possessions, is itself sinful. This is a mistake.

The Bible in fact commands us to work. "We exhort you, brethren ... to work with your hands, as we charged you; so that you may command the respect of outsiders, and be dependent on nobody" (1 Thess. 4:10-12). First of all Christians must provide for themselves. Those who are idle must be rebuked, whatever the reason for their idleness. "Keep away from any brother who is living in idleness" (2 Thess. 3:6). In this case the reason the believers were not working seems to have been a religious one—they were anticipating the immediate return of Christ and so considered work useless.

Elsewhere, while rebuking those who were not working because they were stealing, Paul points to a further reason why the individual should work. "Let the thief no longer steal, but rather let him labor, doing honest work with his hands, so that he may be able to give to those in need" (Eph. 4:28). That a person who has something as a result of work should be careful to share it with "those in need" is stressed frequently in the New Testament. And in our materialistic culture in the West today it is imperative that we echo this emphasis and challenge one another to greater giving and less materialism. The danger, though, in one's contempt for the level of materialism both inside the church and outside it, is to strike against possessions as such. This we must not do for the Bible defends the legitimacy of possessions.

But the Bible also singles out two great dangers concerning possessions: materialism and selfishness. For example, in the Sermon on the Mount, Jesus warns his disciples: "Do not lay up for yourselves treasures on earth" (Mt. 6:19), and again, "You cannot serve God and mammon" (6:24). And Paul warns: "Those who desire to be rich fall into temptation, into a snare, into many senseless and hurtful desires that plunge men into ruin and destruction. For the love of money is the root of all evils" (1 Tim. 6:9-10).

But such statements must not be read as if they exclude possessions. Interestingly, in this same passage (1 Tim. 6: 9-10) Paul indicates that there are rich people in the church. He does not condemn them for their riches. Instead, he warns them about both materialism and selfishness. First, he warns them not to have their lives controlled by their possessions. "As for the rich in this world, charge them not to be haughty, nor to set their hopes on uncertain riches but on God who richly furnishes us with everything to enjoy" (6:17). Possessions must never become the focus of attention in our lives. They must not become our master. "You cannot serve God and mammon." We must not "serve the creature" (Rom. 1:23, 25), which for the West today is more likely to mean wealth than the worship of idols (though there is no essential difference). Second, he urges them to use their possessions unselfishly. "They are to do good, to be rich in good deeds, liberal and generous" (1 Tim. 6:18).

Another passage sometimes used to defend the view that Christianity excludes either possessions or riches is the account of the rich ruler (Lk. 18:18-30):

> And a ruler asked him, "Good Teacher, what shall I do to inherit eternal life?" And Jesus said to him, "Why do you call me good? No one is good but God alone. You know the commandments: 'Do not commit adultery, Do not kill, Do not steal, Do not bear false witness, Honor your father and mother.' " And he said, "All these I have observed from my youth." And when Jesus heard it, he said to him, "One thing you still lack. Sell all that you have and distribute to the poor, and you will have treasure in heaven; and come, follow me." But when he heard this he became sad, for he was very rich. Jesus looking at him said, "How hard it is for those who have riches to enter the kingdom of God! For it is easier for a camel to go through the eye of a needle than for a rich man to enter the kingdom of God." Those who heard it said, "Then who can be saved?" But he said, "What is impossible with men is possible with God." And Peter said, "Lo, we have left our homes and followed you." And he said to them, "Truly, I say to you, there is no man who has left house or wife or brothers or parents or children, for the sake of the kingdom of God, who will not receive manifold more in this time, and in the age to come eternal life."

Jesus' command that the rich man go and sell all that he has must be read in the light of his general observations later. After the man had gone away sorrowful, Jesus said, "How hard it is for those who have riches to enter the kingdom of God!" This rich man was faced with the choice to have a dif-

ferent center for his life, a different integration point than he had had previously. This is of course the choice for anyone—to turn from whatever has been the center (another God, a religious system, a person, or things) to the living God of the Bible. And it is never an easy choice.

In this encounter with the wealthy ruler, Jesus is emphasizing that possessions—especially great possessions—constitute a real pull away from a proper submission to God. Evidently, the rich ruler was trying to have his cake *and* eat it too, seeming to acknowledge God's authority without in fact acknowledging it at the center of his life—his possessions. For the ruler says, "All these [the commandments cited by Jesus as the religious duty of one who desires to do what God requires] I have observed from my youth." But Jesus unmasks his hypocrisy: "One thing you still lack. Sell all that you have and distribute to the poor." This is the heart of the story: God must be at the center of our lives. In whatever way we may be rich, whether in possessions or in talent, we face the struggle to set aside these things and to be "rich toward God" (Lk. 12:21). The refusal to be generous with one's wealth and possessions, home and time always lays bare a devotion to mammon.

One more passage will help to show that the New Testament does not prohibit possessions but insists on the right use of them. Let us consider the example of the early church in Jerusalem. "And all who believed were together and had all things in common; and they sold their possessions and goods and distributed them to all, as any had need" (Acts 2:44-45). Further on we are told specifically:

Now the company of those who believed were of one heart and soul, and no one said that any of the things which he possessed was his own, but they had everything in common.... There was not a needy person among them, for as many as were possessors of lands or houses sold them, and brought the proceeds of what was sold and laid it at the apostles' feet; and distribution was made to each as any had need. (Acts 4:32, 34-35)

There are several things to notice here. The practice in the Jerusalem church of "having everything in common" did not mean that members were *obligated* to give up whatever they possessed or that they did in fact give up all their possessions. This is made clear by the experience of Ananias and Sapphira recorded in Acts 5. This couple had deceived the church by pretending that all the proceeds from the sale of a piece of property had been given to the church for distribution among those who had need, when in fact only a portion had been given. It was the deceit which constituted the wrong, not the fact that they had sold only a part of their property. The property did not have to be sold, for, as Peter said, "While it remained unsold, did it not remain your own?" In saying this he establishes the legitimacy of possessions. Moreover, even when the property was sold the proceeds did not have to be given away in their entirety: "And after it was sold, was it not at your disposal?" The wrong was that they sinned in saying they had given the whole when in fact they had "kept back some of the proceeds."

Elsewhere in Acts and throughout the New Testament there are indications that Christians continued to own property. Christians owned homes (1 Cor. 16:19; Rom. 16:5; Acts 18:7; Philem. 2), engaged in business (Acts 16:14), and even owned slaves (though Paul made clear that in Christ each person is of equal dignity [Gal. 3:28] and insisted that Philemon should take back his runaway slave Onesimus, "no longer as a slave but more than a slave, as a beloved brother" [Philem. 16]). What is also obvious from the New Testament as a whole is that there were considerable differences in wealth among the members of a particular congregation (see Eph. 6:5-9; Col. 3:22—4:1; 1 Tim. 6:1-2).

So then, while the Jerusalem church was *outstanding* in its desire to use possessions unselfishly, it was not acting on a different principle than is found elsewhere in the New Testament. The principle was uniform—unselfish ownership of possessions.

We have used the issue of possessions to illustrate that

the New Testament never advocates an abandonment of the physical. Sin is never confused with the physical even though it involves the physical. Even in the acquisition of wealth which, as Paul says, is at the root of so much evil, the Bible is quite clear in distinguishing between sin and the self. The self can and must be involved in the acquisition and possession of property but that does not make it sinful. The sin arises from the misuse of the physical.

Affirming the Self and Suffering with Christ

Another group of passages in the New Testament appear to advocate the negation of the self.

Then Jesus told his disciples, "If any man would come after me, let him deny himself and take up his cross and follow me. For whoever would save his life will lose it, and whoever loses his life for my sake will find it." (Mt. 16: 24-25)

Do not think that I have come to bring peace on earth; I have not come to bring peace, but a sword. (Mt. 10:34)

[Paul and Barnabas] returned . . . strengthening the souls of the disciples . . . saying that through many tribulations we must enter the kingdom of God. (Acts 14:21-22)

While we live we are always being given up to death for Jesus' sake. . . . So death is at work in us. (2 Cor. 4:11-12)

You endured a hard struggle with sufferings. (Heb. 10:32)

It has been granted to you that for the sake of Christ you should not only believe in him but also suffer for his sake. (Phil. 1:29)

All these passages deal with the problem of the two humanities—those who are "in Christ" and those who are not "in Christ." The believer is hated for Christ's sake. "Because you are not of the world . . . therefore the world hates you" (Jn. 15:19).

In some form or other, not necessarily through public or physical persecution only, believers are divided from unbelievers. We accept this division because, since the Fall, humankind is in opposition to God. We accept it but do not consider it ideal. It makes us sorrowful just as it did Jesus. Hatred for God is unwarranted, as Jesus said, "They hated me without a cause" (Jn. 15:25). This is the most tragic aspect of a now tragic world. God desires to save men, but they reject his love. Therefore, although believers weep over this division, we should not be surprised at suffering which goes with it (1 Pet. 4:12). Since we belong to Christ and he was rejected by the world, we too will be rejected.

Far from encouraging such a rejection, however, Christians should seek to live peaceably with everyone (Rom. 12:18). We must love all those around us and not just other Christians, even though we have a special relationship of love with "those who are of the household of faith" (Gal. 6:10). We must accept separation from the world but we must not glory in it.

If we suffer as a result of this "sword" (Mt. 10:34), we must make certain we are not suffering for wrongdoing, but only for righteousness' sake (Mt. 5:10-11; 1 Pet. 2:20).

In Matthew 16:21 Jesus tells his disciples that he is going to suffer and die. Peter discourages him. Whereupon Jesus tells them that just as he is faced with the choice to keep his life or lose it, they are too. They must decide whether to side with the humanity which owns God or with the humanity which disowns him. It is to this ordeal that the passages above refer.

In saying that they must be prepared to take up their cross, Jesus did not mean that they would necessarily die. That was what it meant for him. But for his disciples it means principally the willingness to do the will of God even if it means separation from others, rejection by the world. That we need to be willing to take up the cross *daily* indicates that Jesus is not calling principally for martyrdom (though that may be the end result) but for separation. This is never easy, but it is what being a follower of Jesus entails. Therefore the attitude needs to be renewed day by day. The experience of oneness which believers rightly esteem (see pp. 22-24) they must be prepared to forego. If unity with others comes at the cost of denying Jesus, then we must be prepared to forego safety, comfort, respect and even life itself.

The denial may even include a refusal to be identified with the members of one's own household: "If any one comes to me and does not hate his own father and mother and wife and children and brothers and sisters, yes, and even his own life, he cannot be my disciple" (Lk. 14:26). This is clearly not intended to be taken literally as shown by Christ's care of Mary as he was on the cross. Rather, this denial speaks of our need for a devotion to Christ, greater than the desire for togetherness with the rest of humanity and even one's own family.

How is it, then, that an experience which evidently includes pain and sorrow is not a negation? Only when it is set in the total framework of life as presented by the Bible. We do not live in the materialist's universe—a universe of matter only. In the materialist's universe life is meaningless and the end of life is death. But in the biblical view, life is eternal, an experience which even in the present is not all ugliness and sorrow, and certainly will not be so in the future. At his second coming, Christ will restore all things and "wipe away every tear" from our eyes (Rev. 21:4).

This immediately changes our perspective. When we see that we are creatures of *eternal* significance, even our present negative experiences are meaningful. Death is not the end of life; nor are the achievements of this life overwhelmed by the grave. On the contrary, they have value even to the extent of being related to our life beyond the grave (see chapter ten). Whatever good we forfeit in the present (for example, the enjoyment of family or friends or life itself) is not ultimate loss, for as Paul says, "This slight momentary affliction is preparing for us an eternal weight of glory beyond all comparison . . . for the things that are seen are transient, but the things that are unseen are eternal" (2 Cor. 4:17-18).

This glory is being prepared for us by God because we have

identified ourselves with the Son of God: we have moved from the kingdom of darkness to the kingdom of light. In so doing, we have dissociated ourselves from "the world" and from "the unfruitful works of darkness" (Eph. 5:11) and consequently find ourselves in conflict with the world.

We must not pretend that the suffering due to hostility from the world is not real. The denial of the self is real denial, the separation is real, the sorrow is real, the suffering is real, the death is real. But it is not an overwhelming loss "for we know that if the earthly tent we live in is destroyed, we have a building from God, a house not made with hands, eternal in the heavens" (2 Cor. 5:1).

Implicit in the believer's willingness to "lose his life," to deny self, to "hate his life" is the conviction that life has such eternal significance that it is better to forego the acceptance and the approval of others in the present than to compromise or adulterate that significance. Can any affirmation of life be greater than this? This is not acting against the self, though it may seem so to the outsider who is judging by appearances only. The things "the world" considers normal and necessary the Christian is ready to lose—job, friends, family, even life. Surely this is madness. Surely this is hatred of life.

But is it? Christians prize work, friendship, love within the family and all things good and beautiful because they are part of God's creation. They have inherent value and are not to be rejected. But at the same time Christians are prepared to forego the pleasures involved in each of these things because they affirm that there is a real difference between good and evil, morality and immorality, light and darkness. This difference overarches the things of this world and alone guarantees their value, and exists whether we accept it or not, because God's character remains the moral basis of the universe. Nothing will remove him or change him. In conversion a sinful person acknowledges this to be the case, acknowledges that he deserves judgment, and then flees for refuge to Christ.

It is the certainty of an eternal significance to life which underlies our actions, both in fleeing to Christ for salvation and subsequently in being prepared (though not seeking it or idealizing it) to be hated by the world for Christ's sake. "For what will it profit a man, if he gains the whole world and forfeits his life?" (Mt. 16:26). Therefore, "whoever loses his life for my sake will find it" (Mt. 16:25). Jesus' followers are prepared to suffer, to take up the cross daily, not because they despise life but because they see a deeper significance to life than mere physical existence.

Affirming the Self and Redeeming the World

In this section we want to deal with those passages which indicate that it is not only possible, but right for a Christian to forego experiences which are legitimate in themselves. There is an overlap here with the previous section. The experience of family-love is legitimate, so is the experience of friendship, and these experiences, we have said, the Christian must be ready to "lose" when the need arises, that is whenever he is "hated for Christ's sake." Now we want to consider other passages which speak of losing oneself in the context of redeeming the world. Once again a negative attitude toward life seems to be implied.

By *redeeming the world* we do not mean that a Christian redeems the world as Christ redeems the world. The distinction is absolute: only Christ died for the sins of humanity; he is the only Savior, the only one through whom forgiveness is possible. "There is salvation in no one else, for there is no other name under heaven given among men by which we must be saved" (Acts 4:12). In this sense Christ's work of redemption is unique.

Nevertheless, the Bible makes clear that believers are involved in God's work of redemption since they are representatives of Christ now that he has ascended to be with the Father. So Paul describes himself as an "ambassador for Christ." Though as an apostle he has special authority, he includes his colleagues as he writes, "We are ambassadors for Christ, God making his appeal through us" (2 Cor. 5:20).

He emphasizes in 1 Corinthians 3:5-15 that the one who works is not to be glorified for as he says, "Only God . . . gives the growth. . . . You are God's field, God's building" (3:7, 9). Yet the other element is also present and must not be lost while stressing God's activity. As a worker for God, the Christian is a significant colaborer in the work of reconciliation.

Colossians 1:24-29 teaches the same thing: Paul says, "In my flesh I complete what is lacking in Christ's afflictions for the sake of his body." He certainly cannot mean that Christ's work of atonement is incomplete, for his repeated emphasis is that man is saved *only* through the work of Christ and that therefore nothing can be added to it. What he means is simply that Christ did not endure all the suffering which was to be suffered by those who are members of his kingdom. Christ's suffering for sin as the Lamb of God can be shared by no one else; but suffering for the sake of righteousness is something which all believers are called to share with him. "For as we share abundantly in Christ's sufferings, so through Christ we share abundantly in comfort too" (2 Cor. 1:5-6).

Before Christ came, believers in the Old Testament had suffered for the sake of God's truth. Hebrews 11:26 even describes Moses' suffering as "abuse suffered for the Christ." Since Christ's death, believers have suffered as well. In neither case is salvation achieved by the individual's suffering, for it is by Christ's work only that people are saved.

Yet the believers' suffering is significant for believers share in Christ's redemptive work. The world continues to be lost and in darkness. Christ came to rescue the world and, through his unique work, made such a rescue possible. Nevertheless, the Christian is involved in completing it by striving to see Christ's work of redemption made known and appropriated. Only in this sense was Christ's suffering incomplete.

It follows, then, that just as Christ's redemptive work involved the laying aside of certain experiences legitimate in themselves, so the believer's work of applying that redemption involves personal loss of the same kind. Paul puts it this way: "Your attitude should be the same as that of Christ Jesus: Who, being in very nature God, did not consider equality with God something to be grasped, but made himself nothing, taking the very nature of a servant" (Phil. 2: 5-7 NIV). What Christ was laying aside was not something evil in itself—far from it. Nor was he compelled to lay it aside; he chose to. He did it because he was looking "to the interests of others." So Paul urges the believers in Philippi to have a similar attitude. Let each of you look not only to your own interests; but also to the interests of others" (Phil. 2:4).

Notice, by the way, that Paul admits a degree of self-interest. He says, "Look not only to your own interests. . . ." Concern for the things of one's own life is both necessary and valid. One cannot exist for example without providing oneself with food; a farmer must seek to make his own fields fruitful; a businesswoman must be concerned about the interest of her own business, and so on. This is not automatically selfishness. But it must be balanced with an equal emphasis on the interests of others. So the commandment, "You shall love your neighbor as yourself" (Mt. 22:39), means that one must be as concerned about one's neighbor as one is about oneself.

But another set of delicate and difficult questions arises. We live in a lost world, we are part of a fallen humanity. On every hand spiritual and physical needs, near at hand as well as distant, cry out for attention. In which direction does the Christian choose to move? Are the needs at hand more important than the needs far away, or vice versa? Care must be taken not to produce a continuous state of guilt. Every experience can be a source of self-recrimination: "Here I am eating this food when someone else is hungry," "Here I am in a comfortable bed when many are homeless" or "Here I am indulging in a luxury, going to a concert, when the money could have been used for those in physical need or for the spread of the gospel." Such guilt comes easily to any who feel deeply the needs of the world.

The opposite tendency, however, must also be guarded against. We are sinners still and, being selfish, we know only too well how to take care of our own interests. So exhortations to consider the interests of others, feed the hungry, heal the sick, look after orphans and widows in their distress, visit those in prison and so on, are also necessary and Scripture is full of them.

How can we fulfill our responsibility to care for others, without allowing this responsibility to become oppressive? When is it right to give away money and when is it right to keep it? When is it right to take the energy and time to help someone who is going through a difficult experience psychologically, and when is it right instead to sit by the fire at home and read a book?

The most important thing to say is that there are no rules for such conduct. Scripture does not give us any, nor should we as Christians try to establish any. It is a serious mistake to do so. Rather, what we must do is present with equal stress the two principles mentioned about: on the one hand, the validity of a proper interest in one's own experience and, on the other, the need to see and take care of the needs of others. There are no easy or permanent solutions here. Each believer, as a steward, is responsible only to God—not to others. As Paul says, "Do not pronounce judgement about a person's stewardship . . . before the Lord comes. . . . Then every man will receive his commendation from God" (1 Cor. 4:5). Also, as situations change, the application of the two principles will vary. The individual must work this out before God.

However, because we must be ruled by the principle of loving others around us, we must be prepared to give ourselves away. That is what love means. As Paul says, "Christ loved me and gave himself for me." And in imitation of that attitude, Paul says of himself, "I will most gladly spend and be spent for your souls" (2 Cor. 12:15). So, out of concern for others, believers must be prepared to forego experiences which in themselves are legitimate. Where this is absent, it is possible that faith is dead (Jas. 2:14-17), and certainly Christ's name is dishonored. Where it is present, it is the living demonstration of the truth of Jesus' words and works (Jn. 13:35; 17:23). The world cannot be redeemed apart from suffering of this sort.

Many passages in the New Testament illustrate this principle. Mark 6:31, for example, says that Jesus was prepared to spend himself so that even his eating was affected: "Many were coming and going, and they had no leisure even to eat." But this same incident shows that rest is legitimate too, for Jesus, because of the pressures on them all, directs the disciples to "come away . . . to a lonely place, and rest a while." The disciples were not to feel guilty because they were leaving the needs of the people and going to rest. Yet, when Jesus and the disciples arrived at the place they had chosen for their rest, there was a great throng and Jesus "had compassion on them, because they were like sheep without a shepherd" (6:34). Once again, their interests came before his own.

Even more radical is Jesus' statement that some lay aside marriage out of concern for this principle: "There are eunuchs who have made themselves eunuchs for the sake of the kingdom of heaven" (Mt. 19:12). Paul echoes this in 1 Cor. 7: 32-34: "I want you to be free from anxieties. The unmarried man is anxious about the affairs of the Lord, how to please the Lord; but the married man is anxious about worldly affairs, how to please his wife, and his interests are divided."

Here too balance and caution are necessary. Two mistakes can be made about celibacy. The first is to think that celibacy is superior to marriage. Paul's comments here must be read in the light of his contextual statement in 7:26 ("because of the present crisis"). He is clearly not making celibacy a norm as can be seen both from 1 Corinthians 7 itself and from what he says elsewhere about marriage.[1] Second, it is equally a mistake to see no virtue in celibacy. Because the center of man's experience is not sex, it is possible for men and women to be fulfilled as persons outside marriage, even though this is not the norm. It is a particular calling, an extraordinary gift. As such, it has real value. (We will look specifically at marriage in chapter nine.)

For the Sake of the Gospel

Many other passages indicate the importance and appropriateness of self-sacrifice. Paul says, for example, that, as an apostle, he has a right to be supported by the church. But he worked to support himself, saying, "We have not made use of this right, but we endure anything rather than put an obstacle in the way of the gospel of Christ" (1 Cor. 9:12). He foregoes something which is legitimate and even has the sanction of God's law (1 Cor. 9:8-11) out of concern to put no obstacle in anyone's way. He suffers toil and trouble which he need not suffer.

Paul mentions other ways in which this principle moves him ... "though I am free from all men, I have made myself a slave to all, that I might win the more." Without compromising the message of the gospel in any way he chooses to lay aside certain practices which are not wrong in themselves. So "to the Jews I became as a Jew ... to those outside the law I became as one outside the law ... I have become all things to all men. ... I do it all for the sake of the gospel" (1 Cor. 9:19-23).

Paul endured toil and hardship not required of him for the sake of the gospel. It is in this light that we must understand his references to the difficult experiences he has been through (2 Cor. 6:4-10; 10:13-16). He is not boasting. He is pointing to experiences which indicate that he has loved others. By this he has shown the reality of his commitment to "spend and be spent" for them.

This attitude—the willingness to give oneself away, to give up *good* things for the sake of better—appears at first sight to be negative but is in fact positive. It is the affirmation of one's true, human identity. The "unnatural" existence, the denial of one's true identity, is the self-centered existence.

Some measure of this reality must be present in every believer. The degree is not the central issue, and care must be taken that this never becomes a principle of self-glorification or a basis on which to condemn others who have not spent themselves to the same degree (1 Cor. 4:5). But the church and the individual ignore this principle at their peril. We are to be concerned about this principle of giving ourselves away not only because the law of God states that we should love in this way, and not only because Scripture points us to Christ as our great example (though both are true), but because that is in fact what love means, and what in fact we were created to do. It is our nature. Only as we learn to live in this new way will we be fulfilled.

So even the idea of giving up or losing something is loss only in a limited sense. On the one hand it is real loss because what we lay aside in redeeming the world is in fact laid aside—time to enjoy an artistic talent, to read a book or to make a garden. This is not insignificant. At times it causes great longing and heart-searching and is a source of temptation just as the devil used life itself to tempt Jesus when Peter said, "This [suffering] shall never happen to you" (Mt. 16:22). We must not underestimate this loss.

Yet in another sense we lose nothing. We do not experience *only* loss now, for God honors the imitation of his love. When Peter said that he and the other disciples had left everything to follow him, Jesus replied,

There is no one who has left house or brothers or sisters or mother or father or children or lands, for my sake and for the gospel, who will not receive a hundredfold *now in this time,* houses and brothers and sisters and mothers and children and lands, with persecutions, and in the age to come eternal life. (Mk. 10:29-30)

Paul says, "You will be enriched in every way for great generosity" (2 Cor. 9:11). And elsewhere he assures us that "whatever good anyone does, he will receive the same again from the Lord" (Eph. 6:8). Moreover, we do not suffer an ultimate loss for God "is preparing for us an eternal weight of glory beyond all comparison" (2 Cor. 4:17).

We ought, therefore, to be careful as we come across passages in the New Testament which appear to give a negative slant to the Christian life. Negative they may be, in that they involve the eradicating of what is wrong or the enduring of persecution or the laying aside of pleasurable and legitimate experiences. But when seen in the context of the biblical view of humanity, the negative element fades away and these experiences, though painful, are seen to be positive—the recovery and the expression of our true identity and dignity.

THE MIND

SEVEN

Often in our discussion, the mind and its part in living and knowing God has arisen. We have seen how the influence of Platonism engendered among many Christians a negative attitude toward the body and the mind. Modern developments too have affected Christians' thinking about the mind and its relation to spiritual things. We shall now consider some of these developments.

Skepticism

One of the prominent features of the modern scientific culture of which we are a part is that it tends to doubt religious statements. To speak of God or of miracles or of life after death is to speak of things which are unprovable. Because they are not accessible to science, it is claimed, they cannot be true. Dr. Edmund Leach expresses this attitude well. "Our idea of God is a product of history. What I now believe about the supernatural is derived from what I was taught by my parents, and what they taught me was derived from what they were taught, and so on. But such beliefs are justified by faith alone, never by reason, and the true believer is expected to go on reaffirming his faith in the same verbal formula, even if the passage of history and the growth of scientific knowledge should have turned the words into plain nonsense."[1]

But this skepticism was the result not of "the growth of scientific knowledge," as Leach suggests, but of the philosophic revolution of the eighteenth century.[2] What the Enlightenment philosophers were concerned to do was to overthrow any religious view of reality.[3] They rejected the idea of revelation and replaced it with human reason as the only reliable authority.[4] It was this rejection of a supernatural world view which gave rise to the skepticism that surrounds us today.

Immanuel Kant, for example, responding to the skepticism of David Hume, constructed a theory of knowledge which excluded the possibility of knowing God with the mind.[5] D. F. Strauss wrote a "life of Jesus" in 1836 in which he argued that "the supernatural element in the Gospels was a 'myth' entirely without historical foundation."[6] In the natural sciences the idea spread that every advance of knowledge meant necessarily that Christianity was deprived of some of its truth and that step by step God was removed from the scheme of things.

In the nineteenth century, a growing number of intellectuals believed that reason had exposed religion for what it was—superstition. It was felt that no reasonable person, making proper use of the mind, could accept the Santa Claus-like details of, say, the Incarnation and resurrection. Adolf Harnack, a prominent German theologian at the end of the nineteenth century, dogmatically asserted that "miracles . . . do not happen."[7] And in Nietzsche's *Thus Spoke Zarathustra,* the hero marveled that the religious man had not yet heard that God was dead.[8]

Skepticism gradually developed until by the early part of

the twentieth century the rout of Christianity seemed complete. Whole disciplines, such as sociology, psychology and anthropology, were spawned by the new philosophy. In these new disciplines it was felt that religious ideas bore no relation to objective truth; religion was simply the product of history. The churches fared no better: skepticism about the historical reliability of the Bible was as great within them as outside them.[9]

The problem which confronted evangelicals, therefore, was the problem of truth. Was all that they believed really true? Was it true just in their experience, that is, because it made them feel or act better? Or was it also an accurate statement about the universe in which they were living? Did God create everything at the beginning? Was Adam a historical person? Did the Fall as described in Genesis 3 actually take place? And with the intellectual giants of the culture almost unanimously opposed to these ideas, how could evangelicals seriously maintain that their faith was reasonable?

It was an outstanding feature of evangelicalism that it resisted the influence of the Enlightenment. Though the culture as a whole, including even the majority of all Protestant denominations, adopted its skeptical attitude toward the Bible, the evangelicals stood firm. They doubted neither the supernatural elements nor the historical and scientific details. This was in fact its distinctive characteristic as over against the Protestant liberalism which emerged from Germany in the nineteenth century.

At the same time, however, many, rather than defending the reasonableness of Christianity (as others have done[10]), granted the unreasonableness of their faith,[11] divorced faith from reason and adopted a suspicious, negative attitude toward the mind. Some have suggested, for example, that the mind is only a hindrance to faith, that it gets in the way of a person becoming a Christian and plays an insignificant role in the growth of a Christian. Others have even defended such an attitude by referring to Paul's argument in the first two chapters of 1 Corinthians (see pp. 148-53).

Reason Challenged

Skepticism, however, was not the only child of the Enlightenment nor were rational doubts the only problems with which evangelicals had to deal. Reaction set in and reason was challenged even among those who made no claims to religious faith. The virtues and achievements of the mind began to be questioned. Some were dismayed by the inability of "enlightened" humanity to bring about peace and good will. Others were threatened by the encroachments of machinery. Still others grieved over technology's rape of nature. Many despaired of meaning within an impersonal universe.[12]

Hence, reason was simultaneously exalted and disparaged. Some said the Bible was untrue because it *conflicted with* the assured results of science. Others said that religious "truth" and consequently the truth of the Bible *had nothing to do with* scientific or historical accuracy. So the rationalists derided the idea that the Bible was both philosophically and scientifically true. At the same time, those who maintained that religion was for the heart only, that the mind was inappropriate for understanding truth, criticized the evangelicals for holding tenaciously to the scientific and philosophic truth of the Bible. During the past hundred years, then, evangelicals have felt threatened from both sides—and on neither side has the struggle been easy.

Here is not one Goliath to fight, but two. One can understand why Christians have trembled and become disheartened, for these two attitudes which are so opposed to the historic Christian position constitute the overwhelming consensus in the West today.

Faced with this opposition, many Christians have retreated from a defense both of the reasonableness of Christianity and of the importance of the mind. But if humanity was created with a mind, why is the mind now set aside? What is the Bible's principal teaching on the subject?

First of all, the Bible itself justifies no such withdrawal. For example, when Paul made his defense before Festus the

Roman governor, his language was striking: "I am not insane.... What I am saying is true and reasonable [*sophrosúne*]" (Acts 26:25 NIV). Arndt and Gingrich in their Greek Lexicon give the meaning of *sophrosúne* as "reasonableness, rationality." So Paul claims that Christianity is reasonable, rational—in other words, that it makes sense of the whole of human experience.

The Validity of the Mind

By rational we generally mean "in accord with reason." When A says, "A circle is square," B automatically objects that circles cannot be square. This seems rather obvious but it is important. Similarly, if we said at this moment as you are reading these words in English, "You are reading Chinese," our statement would be untrue. There are certain set patterns of thought in our minds which enable us to determine the rightness or wrongness of propositions. What determines the shape or pattern of the "internal standards" cannot be explained by us; it is simply part of our humanness, of being made in the image of God. But to deny that we think this way leads ultimately to a loss of distinction between reality and fantasy, and, if pursued to its end, to madness and the loss of any meaningful communication.

Therefore, when any proposition (whether "religious" or "scientific") is made which claims to be true, reason tests whether or not it is true. This it does in two ways—first, by examining the self-consistency of the proposition and, second, by seeing whether it agrees with other knowledge of reality. In other words, there have to be two levels of consistency for any statement to be true. Internal consistency requires that ideas within Christianity not contradict each other, and external consistency demands that Christianity not contradict genuine historical and scientific knowledge.

Although the faculty of reason has continued to be a part of all human experience despite the Fall, we have been unable to discover the whole truth about ourselves and the universe. This is due, in part, to our separation from God who alone is able to give definitive answers to the basic questions about the nature of reality and, in part, to the fact that our character (thinking as well as behavior) has become distorted. But this distortion does not mean that reason is useless, for our whole experience—every conversation, every simple task we perform—is possible only because of the validity of reason.

Despite this basic importance of reason, there is an area in which reason is helpless, namely our sinfulness. Jonathan Edwards explains why only the message of the Bible gives us a solution to that:

> Such are our circumstances now in our fallen state, that nothing which it is needful for us to know concerning God, is manifest by the light of nature, in the manner in which it is necessary for us to know it. For the knowledge of no truth in divinity (i.e. Christian divinity) is of significance to us, any otherwise than as it some way or other belongs to the gospel-scheme, or as it relates to a Mediator. But the light of nature teaches us no truth in this matter.... It is only the Word of God, contained in the Old and New Testament, which teaches us Christian divinity.[13]

Edwards is careful to stress that the mind is not unimportant. Yet its value is limited, since in the most important issue—redemption—it is completely dependent on God's revelation.

This being so, it would be tempting to discard the mind, particularly when speaking to someone who is asking whether Christianity is true. The New Testament does not allow this, however. The non-Christian is capable of understanding what God has said. Though this obviously is not just a physical process, comprehension must include hearing the words of the gospel and understanding them. God approaches people on the basis of the validity of the mind. If they do not respond, God holds them responsible. The truth is clear; to avoid it people must suppress it. As Paul says, "For what can be known about God is plain to them, because God has shown it to them. Ever since the creation of the world his invisible nature ... has been clearly perceived in the things that have been made. So they are without excuse" (Rom. 1:19-20). They are without excuse not just morally but intellectually.

Some will respond at this point that it is the work of the Holy Spirit to give an understanding of the truth, to give discernment between what is true and what is false. This is true, but it must be carefully qualified. First, the work of the Holy Spirit in enlightening an individual's mind is a secret work, neither visible to nor controlled by humans. Also, this fact of the Holy Spirit's work does not negate the use of reason either before or after regeneration. From the start, the gospel must be presented as true, as something that will commend itself to reason. As J. Gresham Machen has said, "We must do our utmost to give people good reasons why they should believe, but it is the Holy Spirit who opens their minds to attend to the evidence."[14]

Others will insist that an appeal to the reason is not the most important thing in presenting the gospel. Although winning intellectual arguments is not the key to evangelism, some information about the content of Christianity must be communicated in order for anyone to become a Christian.

What we have seen in our culture is that disregard for the mind can produce an evangelism that is merely technique. This is dehumanizing both to speaker and to hearer. Personal evangelism should be characterized by sensitivity. One is talking to another person, not into a tape recorder. The Bible nowhere gives a code for evangelism. The most one can say is that from explicit statements and from instances of personal evangelism in the Bible, it is clear that certain things ought to be present as one tries to help another to faith.

First, our whole life should corroborate the truth of the gospel. This should be evident particularly in our attitude to other people. Though we will always be far from the ideal, we should strive to give this factor in the Bible's teaching its proper emphasis: "Let your manner of life be worthy of the gospel of Christ" (Phil. 1:27). "Let your light so shine before men, that they may see your good works and give glory to your Father who is in heaven" (Mt. 5:16).

Second, we must pray, with Paul, that God will "open . . . a door for the word" (Col. 4:3) and that he will enable us to speak clearly (Col. 4:4) and boldly (Eph. 6:19). We are not engaged in a human enterprise—merely "communicating the gospel." We are engaged in something which is an impossibility for us—to save sinners. This is why Jesus said (in answer to the question "Then who can be saved?"), "What is impossible with men is possible with God" (Lk. 18:26-27). Therefore, we must pray.

Third, there should be a clear statement of the truth. Without knowing a great deal about the Bible or about contemporary objections to it, we may yet declare very simply what the gospel is. The power is in the gospel, not in clever minds or clever answers. As Paul says, the gospel "is the power of God for salvation" (Rom. 1:16). If this is forgotten, the danger of concentrating on one's own ability rather than on the content of God's Word increases.

Finally, there should be a conviction that Christianity is true. Though it is possible to declare the truth while knowing little about it, believers should never consider ignorance a virtue, but always seek to understand what Christianity is and how it relates to contemporary ideas. In this way we grow as Christians and become better able to help others see both what is wrong in alternative systems of thought which deny God and also the truth revealed in the Bible. The very fact that truth exists will be a source of wonder and excitement, and this will be communicated too.[15]

As this happens the division between religious and nonreligious topics of conversation disappears. Since almost everything one talks about necessarily relates in some way or other to the biblical world view, conversations will tend to lead toward the discussion of the basic truths of the Christian faith without any artificial manipulation. Christians may still feel ashamed of the gospel, but gradually, as experience and knowledge grow, Christians should be more and more certain about their view of reality. We have nothing to fear intellectually; it is other world views which are false, and demonstrably so.[16] Therefore, we ought to be able to echo Paul's words, "I am not ashamed of the gospel" (Rom. 1:16). We can then be quite open about our convictions, neither minimizing nor exaggerating the place of argument and intellectual persuasion in bringing a person to believe.

Another result of disregard for the mind in evangelism is an overemphasis on the emotions and the will, as if it were possible to bypass the mind altogether. Because many evangelicals have viewed reason as an enemy of truth and a hindrance to faith, "intellectual questions" have been labeled automatically as a smoke screen designed to obscure the central issue of self-commitment. Undoubtedly, intellectual questions are often used in this way. One can also agree that the ultimate issue in faith is not the mind but the will—the readiness of the individual to humbly acknowledge the Word and the work of the living God. But legitimate questions deserve answers.

Many evangelicals, however, give the impression that there is a conflict between the mind and faith. Not surprisingly, this has led to an unhealthy emphasis on experience. To the question, "How can you be sure that what you believe is true?" many would answer, "I have experienced it in my heart and therefore know that it is true." Certainly, if the truth is only something we know in our heads, then we are ignoring one of the clearest elements of the Bible's teaching, namely, that the purpose of our creation and salvation is to experience and enjoy a relationship with God.

The problem is not the appeal to experience as such, but that no appeal is made to the objective reasons for the truth of Christianity. Worse, such an appeal is considered by some to be a hindrance. To have an objective defense for the truth

—to appeal, for example, to history and science—involves us in the need to reason, discuss and argue. This would be wrong, according to some, because reason (they say) is a stumbling block to faith. This attitude, serious enough because unbiblical, is additionally serious because it coincides, unhappily, with a similar emphasis in liberal Protestantism.

From the time of the Enlightenment, liberal Protestantism has had an element of irrationalism within it. Schleiermacher, who lived at the same time as Immanuel Kant, introduced a flight from reason which has continued to the present. He said that the seat of faith was not reason but the emotions and the will. Faith was "a matter of individual experience, a personal intuition ... not ... an acceptance of theological propositions."[17] So in this view the doctrines of the Christian faith were considered irrelevant. Certain of them, for example, the resurrection, might be disproved scientifically (since rationalism denied the possibility of miracles) without affecting faith. Religious experience, not statements about the world of history and science, was the source of theology.

Though similar in effect (both lead to commitment based on blind faith), the liberal Protestant dismissal of reason and the evangelical dismissal of reason have quite different backgrounds. Yet nevertheless a similarity between the two exists at the point of the dismissal of reason. Evangelicals said, "The statements in the Bible are true but they have to be accepted in blind faith, in simple commitment, without argument." And liberal Protestants spoke about blind faith and commitment as well.

The difference, of course, was that evangelicals maintained the accuracy of the historical and scientific statements in the Bible: Abraham really did leave a place called Ur, Peter really did betray his Master, and so on. This meant that certain real historical events, in particular the resurrection and ascension which involve the supernatural, had to be believed. The liberal Protestant, on the other hand, re-

fused to be drawn into such a discussion. Whether or not
such events took place was considered irrelevant to faith.
To the liberal Protestant the important thing was commitment to a particular way of life and involvement in certain
experiences—going to church, helping others, becoming
"the man for others."[18] Hence it earned for itself the name
"existential faith."

Certainly faith involves experience and in that sense is
"existential." But in the Bible, "faith" is *true* faith only when
based on the objective truths of Scripture. When these truths
are denied, there may be faith in the sense of a religious or
mystical experience, but it cannot be called Christian
faith.[19]

Truth, Belief and Wisdom

One of the Apostle Paul's principal concerns is to demonstrate the objectivity of the Christian truth. If, in defense of
the gospel, no appeal to objective facts is possible, how can
we be sure that another religion, say Hinduism, for example,
is not preferable to Christianity? This concern is an outstanding feature of all the biblical writers (compare, for example, 2 Pet. 1:16-21).

In Romans 1:18-21 Paul argues that the fact that God is
the creator is evident—"clearly perceived"—in the world.
The evidence is everywhere, even though people do not acknowledge the truth. If people refuse to accept the evidence,
it is because of the hardness of their hearts, because they
"suppress the truth," *not* because the evidence is not clear.
He says the same thing in Ephesians 4:18: "They are dark-
ened in their understanding . . . due to their hardness of
heart." *Hardening of the heart* in Scripture means willful
and inexcusable rejection of the truth.

So Paul's concern is not primarily to get his hearers to
have a religious experience. Instead, he presents them with
the truth, discusses it with them at length (sometimes for
as long as two years, Acts 19:8-10) and urges them to submit themselves to the gospel *because it is true.* So he is con-

cerned with the mind of the nonbeliever.

He is concerned equally with the mind of the believer. The New Testament writers know nothing of a spiritual development separate from the mind. Paul says, "Be transformed by the renewal of your mind" (Rom. 12:2) and Peter says, "Gird up your minds" (1 Pet. 1:13). Christians are to grow in knowledge of the truth and see reality the way God sees it. In order to do that, we must learn, by reading and studying Scripture, where our thinking and attitudes are wrong. Just as the mind is important prior to conversion, it is important for spiritual growth after conversion (see pp. 78-79).

We must here deal with 1 Corinthians 1:17—2:2, for this passage is frequently used to justify disregard for the mind.

Christ did not send me to baptize but to preach the gospel, and not with eloquent wisdom, lest the cross of Christ be emptied of its power. For the word of the cross is folly to those who are perishing, but to us who are being saved it is the power of God. For it is written, "I will destroy the wisdom of the wise, and the cleverness of the clever I will thwart."

Where is the wise man? Where is the scribe? Where is the debater of this age? Has not God made foolish the wisdom of the world? For since, in the wisdom of God, the world did not know God through wisdom, it pleased God through the folly of what we preach to save those who believe. For Jews demand signs and Greeks seek wisdom, but we preach Christ crucified, a stumbling block to Jews and folly to Gentiles, but to those who are called, both Jews and Greeks, Christ the power of God and the wisdom of God. For the foolishness of God is wiser than men, and the weakness of God is stronger than men. (1 Cor. 1:17-25)

And also in 2:1-2 Paul continues, "When I came to you, brethren, I did not come proclaiming to you the testimony of God in lofty words or wisdom. For I decided to know nothing among you except Jesus Christ and him crucified." These are the main sections we need to consider, though Paul's discussion continues through the end of chapter 3.

Sometimes this passage has been read alongside Acts 17. When Paul was in Athens, it is argued, he changed his usual approach while speaking to the philosophers on Mars Hill. Previously he had merely declared the gospel without getting involved in philosophy and intellectual argument. In Athens he tried to meet the pagan philosophers on their own ground. What we find in 1 Corinthians 1—2, it is claimed, is an admission of his mistake, for he had come to Corinth from Athens (see Acts 18:1).

Others understand the passage to mean that the gospel is quite literally folly, that it is bad philosophy and hasn't anything to do with reason. So the Christian's responsibility is simply to declare the gospel, for, it is said, the gospel does not lend itself to argument.

Both of these views reject a reasoned presentation of the gospel. It is this attitude, still quite common among evangelicals, that we want to oppose as vigorously as possible, for Paul could not possibly have been advocating such a view.

Although a detailed exposition of 1 Corinthians 1:17—2:2 is not possible here,[20] we want to outline three principles which must govern any reading of the passage. First, *the text cannot be interpreted to conflict with either 1 Corinthians as a whole or with Romans 1:18-21.* In both letters Paul asserts that Christianity is reasonable. In Romans 1 this is particularly striking: people are guilty before God not first because they are immoral but because they have made inexcusable mistakes in their *thinking*. People have deliberately suppressed the evidence by imagining, for example, that a creature such as a bird or reptile is to be worshiped as divine when its creatureliness is only too apparent (Rom. 1:18-28). It is important to notice here that people are held accountable before God even without reference to special revelation, that is, the Bible.

An inconspicuous but significant evidence of Paul's respect for the mind is the argument in Romans 1—5 which sets out the Christian system in a logical step-by-step fashion. This in itself assumes the validity of reason.

Even in 1 Corinthians 12—14, when discussing the gifts of the Holy Spirit, Paul emphasizes that communications in the church must be in words that will be understandable. "If the bugle gives an indistinct sound, who will get ready for the battle? So with yourselves; if you in a tongue utter speech that is not intelligible, how will any one know what is said?" (1 Cor. 14:8-9). This emphasis upon rational speech is important, for in the very place where one might expect Paul to play down the mind (because of the emphasis on the Holy Spirit) he exalts it.

Second, *Paul does not mean that the gospel is intrinsically foolish*. The Enlightenment objected that Christianity is unreasonable. Some interpret 1 Corinthians 1 to mean that Paul considers Christianity unreasonable. But notice the parallel between the language of 1 Corinthians 1:17-25 and Romans 1:19-22, particularly in the use of the word *foolishness*. 1 Corinthians says that the Greeks "seek wisdom" and look down on the gospel as "foolishness," although this "foolishness of God is wiser than" human wisdom.

> For what can be known about God is plain to them, because God has shown it to them. Ever since the creation of the world his invisible nature, namely, his eternal power and deity, has been clearly perceived in the things that have been made. So they are without excuse. . . . Claiming to be wise, they became fools. (vv. 19-20, 22)

From the sinful human point of view, the gospel is foolish. The Greeks in Athens derided and mocked Paul when he preached the gospel (Acts 17:18, 32) and this is typical of the response of people in general. Before God, however, and from the point of view of the objective truth which surrounds them, it is they who are fools (Rom. 1:22). To deny the truth they must suppress it. The gospel is the "wisdom of God" (1 Cor. 1:24); the alternative philosophies are foolish.

So there is no support in this passage for the idea that Christianity is "bad philosophy." It is the best philosophy. Of course, it is not a philosophy of human construction, and if the word *philosophy* is defined as such then Christianity should not be called a philosophy. But there is value in using the term because Christianity lays claim to the same territory as philosophy, just as rival governments sometimes lay claim to the same geographical area. As one dictionary puts it, most philosophies have been concerned "to ask and answer, in a formal and disciplined way, the great questions of life that ordinary men might put to themselves in reflective moments." And just at the points where each human philosophy must fail (for example, with regard to morality, unity and diversity, and the origin of personality), the Bible has the answers. Whether one chooses to call Christianity a philosophy is immaterial. The important thing is that Christianity is in fact the best and only adequate answer, and therefore in this sense, the best philosophy.

Third, *the expression "the cross of Christ" is not to be read narrowly.* Frequently one hears evangelicals say, "What was sufficient for Paul is sufficient for me—the simple gospel." They then quote from 1 Corinthians 2:2: "I decided to know nothing among you except Jesus Christ and him crucified." By *simple gospel* they mean an unintellectual presentation of the gospel—no reasoning, no mention of philosophy. But this is a serious misinterpretation of Paul's meaning.

He is not here contrasting an intellectual with an unintellectual presentation of the truth. Rather he is contrasting a message which comes solely from God with one which is humanly derived. A parallel idea appears in Colossians 2:8: "See to it that no one makes a prey of you by philosophy and empty deceit." Once again, those who take the view that Christianity is not reasonable leap on such a passage and say, "This supports our position. Paul clearly condemns all philosophy; he condemns any appeal to the mind." But Paul carefully explains what he means by the term *philosophy*. It is philosophy "according to human tradition ... and not according to Christ" (Col. 2:8). He is warning against all philosophies which ignore God's revelation. He is not speaking about philosophy in the sense of the use of the mind or of a reasoned presentation of God's truth.

From what we know of his ministry, both from the book of Acts and his letters, it is evident that Paul was always concerned to make the gospel clear and to express "the whole counsel of God" (Acts 20:27). This is why at one point he describes his work as "taking every thought captive to obey Christ" (2 Cor. 10:4-5). He is not describing conflict within his own mind when he says this. The thoughts he sought to "take captive" were the religious and philosophic ideas of his day which denied God's revealed truth.

Why, then, does he say, "I decided to know nothing among you except Jesus Christ and him crucified" (1 Cor. 2:2)? It is not because he is excluding any other teaching in the Bible, for he repeatedly relates Christ to the Old Testament, to Adam (Rom. 5:12ff), to Abraham (Gal. 3:6-18; 4:21), to Moses and the law (Rom. 7:1-6; Gal. 3:11-13). And he says, all Scripture is God's revelation and therefore important (2 Tim. 3:16). So he cannot be isolating Christ from the rest of Scripture. Nor is he treating *Christ* as a magical word, the very utterance of which gives life to those who hear. It is simply that Christ is the central figure within the Bible. He is concerned to preach "Christ and him crucified" because Christ's person and work of salvation is the focal point of all God's revelation. And in order to do that he deliberately turns away from alternative philosophical ideas which claim to be wise but are in fact foolish.

By preaching only "Christ and him crucified," Paul is also contrasting the power of truth itself with a presentation of the truth which relies on the powers of human persuasion (the techniques of oratory). Paul tries to make the gospel clear, but he carefully avoids attempting to convince by his skill in speaking. In fact, Paul acknowledges that he is "unskilled in speaking" (2 Cor. 11:6), that "his bodily presence is weak, and his speech of no account" (2 Cor. 10:10). Not that Paul does not argue and plead about the kingdom of God (Acts 19:8), but as he speaks he sees the persuasive power in the message itself, the Word of God which is the sword of the Spirit. This is why he sees his reasoning with men as having "divine power to destroy strongholds" (2 Cor. 10:4). When Paul says, "I decided to know nothing among you except Jesus Christ and him crucified," he is saying nothing about how much of the truth should be presented. The presentation of the gospel for Paul is never a narrow thing, a question of simplified techniques. It is the "whole counsel of God"—the person of God, the creation, the Fall, the historical trustworthiness of the Old Testament; the Incarnation, life, death and resurrection of the second person of the Trinity; the return of Christ; the resurrection of the body; and final judgment.

The Mind and the Will
But conversion and spiritual growth are not only through the mind. There is a correlation between being willing to accept and practice God's revealed truth and being able to understand it. People who are unwilling to change either their thinking or habits to accord with what the Bible says, cannot advance spiritually. This is true both in becoming a Christian and in growing as a Christian.

The same principle holds in any area of prejudice. The scientist who is prejudiced against a particular theory will never be able to understand it. He "sees" the truth only when he is prepared to admit that perhaps his own thinking on some fundamental issue is at fault. In personal quarrels also, each party finds it difficult to admit blame; but only as that happens can the relationship be restored. In both examples, simply pointing out the mistake is not enough. Understanding is limited by the degree of willingness to be humble. Intellectual advance is not possible apart from an act of the will.

This personal element is involved in spiritual understanding too. Therefore, it is a mistake to suppose that it is only necessary to instruct the mind. A person's will needs to be challenged not merely *after* the discussion but *within* it. Difficulty in understanding the truth may be due to *unwilling-ness* to understand it. Thus, although the statements of the Bible are objectively true and the evidence clear, a person may not see the truth because of a prejudice against it.

But it must be remembered that Paul was prepared to discuss and reason with those whom he met *not* because he had decided previously that his hearers were "genuine seekers"[21] but because he knew that his statements and the statements of the Old Testament were true. He did not expect his hearers to acknowledge the truth immediately; he was very patient in reasoning with people in the hope that they might "repent and come to know the truth" (2 Tim. 2: 24-26). It is not our place to decide that a person, however obstinate, will not come to repentance.[22]

In stressing the importance of the mind, we are not suggesting that everyone should be approached as if they were university professors or as if the same level of understanding were required of each. It is quite clear that some require to hear more than others before they come to the point of accepting what is presented. Nor are we pleading for the complicated as over against the simple. We are concerned for truth not "intellectualism." If truth is important, then the reasonableness of the truth must be also, as it was to Paul (Acts 26:24-25).

Interestingly enough, the two passages in the book of Acts which tell us about Paul's approach to the gentile world (those who had no contact with God's revelation previously) indicate that Paul very definitely did not shut himself up to a narrow presentation of the truth, the "simple gospel" as some have called it. In Acts 14:15-17 he goes back not immediately to the cross but to the starting point of the gospel — to God's person. Without this backdrop the cross is meaningless. Similarly, in speaking to the Athenian philosophers he first of all shows himself acquainted with their thinking and addresses them on their own ground. And, as in Acts 14, he goes back to God's person and the creation of man in God's image (Acts 17:22-31).

An anti-intellectual view of 1 Corinthians has had a crippling effect on evangelical Christians. The gospel has all too often been reduced to a formula in people's minds. The ABC of the gospel has to be directed at people in no other way than simply ABC—*A* being the fact that people are sinners, *B* that Christ died for them, *C* that all must respond to this and be "committed to Christ." Obviously, our purpose is not to disagree with the meaning of this ABC, nor to say that the gospel should not be presented quite simply in the words of Scripture, or in the order listed above. The glory of Christianity is that it *can* be simply expressed and is able to be understood even by children. What we are saying, however, is that such a presentation is not demanded by Scripture and that insisting on it has played no small part in cutting off evangelicals, unnecessarily, from the rest of society.

This isolation from society is due in part to the evangelical flight from reason, of which we ought to be ashamed. By it we contradict the practice and clear teaching of our Lord and his apostles. "The apostles sought to make an intellectual conquest, to persuade men of the truth of their message, to convince them in order to convert them."[23]

Also we play with fire when we allow the truth of the gospel (and the rational defense of it) to take second place to experience. This would be dangerous at any time. In this moment of history, however, it is lethal since we are surrounded on every side by secular and religious thought which is opposed to the very concept of truth. If our concern is with religious experience at the cost of a strong emphasis on the truth and reasonableness of the biblical record, how shall we be able to oppose the forces arrayed against truth? We shall be like soldiers without arms in the midst of a conflict which, as J. I. Packer says, "is worse than anything since Gnostic theosophy tried to swallow Christianity in the second century."[24]

We call men to submit to Christ, to receive him by faith, only because he and his Scriptures are objectively true. And since we believe them to be true, we must be prepared to join

GUIDANCE

EIGHT

The practical importance of emphasizing humanness in the Christian's life can be seen clearly in the area of guidance. By *guidance* we mean the way Christians discover what they should do—particularly what God wants them to do.

On the one hand, we know only too well the difficulty of deciding on the "right way" for ourselves. There seem to be so many possible directions to go and each is significant and each leads to a completely different life. Also we know ourselves to be fallible and finite; mistakes have been made in the past and can be made again. Often our judgment is clouded by self-interest or fear. Our understanding of things is limited even in the present, and the future is a closed book.

On the other hand, believers know that God is not limited as we are. He sees the whole situation as it is, and the future is open to him as well. We also know that God's attitude toward us is one of kindness and concern, as a father toward his children. God has bound himself by a covenant to lead and protect believers in Jesus and he has the power to do so.

Consequently, we have a natural disinclination to rely on our own understanding, and a natural longing to find out what God sees to be the best way. We often liken God's will to a treasure map: if only, we say, we could get the map, we would know exactly where to go in search of the hidden treasure. We see increasingly, in other words, how necessary and desirable it is to have access to God's "master plan" for our lives. But how do we bring together our need for guidance and God's ability to guide?

No Mechanical Solutions

The great danger here is to erect a mechanical model and seek mechanical solutions. But this is how astrology and fortunetelling devices operate. To do this is to act as if God's guidance were a computer bank into which I could plug and get answers to guidance questions. "Do business on Fridays" or "Do not marry in the first half of the month." With the best intentions in the world we can be operating within a *completely* or a *partially* mechanistic framework.

The completely mechanistic framework involves the issue of God's sovereignty. (This has been discussed already in chapter five, but we must look at it again briefly in this context because so many are confused by it in relation to guidance.) The fact that God is infinite and sovereign over all creation is a teaching of Scripture to which we assent wholeheartedly and with thankfulness. This does not mean, however, that the individual is deprived of responsible action. Because we are made in the image of God, we are able to act responsibly (not just mechanically). Because we are like God, we choose, we love, we create, and so on. This is where the problem arises: how is it possible for a finite person to choose over against an infinite person? Does not the fact of God's infinity mean that everything on the finite level is controlled so that there is no real choice left? Conversely, would it not deprive God of a measure of his infinity to have a finite person able to choose against him? Would it not mean that God's control over what he has created was only tenuous, like someone trying to hold onto a slippery ball?

The Bible tells us such conclusions are unnecessary. God's infinity is not affected by the fact that we are really significant. He does have control over the universe so that the now sinful world will not suddenly spin off into nothingness like a marble rolling off a plate. Yet man is not reduced to a robot as a result. The Bible says emphatically that *both* of these are true.

Our problem intellectually is that we assume the one excludes the other. Therefore we must carefully define in what sense it is, and is not, an "intellectual problem."

This problem stems from the limit of our minds—we cannot see how both can simultaneously be true. Just as our bodies are limited (for example, we cannot be in two places at once), so our minds are limited. Hence it is accurate to say that we cannot understand how sovereignty and responsibility fit together. In this sense Christians do have an "intellectual problem."

But this is not the kind of intellectual problem raised by trying to believe something which is *against* reason. If God is personal and infinite, why is it "against reason" to consider that God has made a finite person? The concept is reasonable, even if we ourselves do not understand how God could construct a finite creature who is free to choose.

Furthermore, this limit to our understanding is not exclusive to the sovereignty/responsibility question. We equally do not understand why humans have only one head and not two, or why pigs should not be able to fly. This is not a unique limitation for the mind.

More importantly, we are not escaping into the irrational when we uphold both God's sovereignty and man's responsibility. On the contrary, what *would* destroy the rationality of Christianity would be the claim that the finite person could, or should be able to, understand God's infinity, thus destroying the finite/infinite distinction—and with it the entire Christian faith.

So, then, to think of sovereignty/responsibility as a problem is a mistake. Far from being a problem, it is yet another magnificent portion of the Christian world view which enables us to live with real meaning. The world is not chaotic, for God is over all; yet within it we are significant.

How does this apply to guidance? The point we are making is that Christians must not erect a mechanical model for seeking God's will. God is not a master computer. The model is wrong. God deals with us *as persons*. So the believer should never be troubled by the idea of making a decision, as if to do so is to encroach on God's territory. Obviously believers *may* become obstinate (like Jonah) and refuse to accept God's guidance. But they need not for this reason disown their ability to decide, as if decisions in and of themselves were dishonoring to God. This is a false antithesis and, if to act like this is commended as a Christian virtue, it is a false religiosity as well. To dishonor our humanness is to dishonor God. To fail to act responsibly often results in foolish decisions and, hence, in sorrow.

Parallel to this is the argument that sinfulness is justification for a total mistrust of human judgment. Our nature is corrupt and, it is claimed, must be superseded by "the divine." Therefore, all guidance must originate completely *outside* ourselves; for example, by means of tongues or by the way circumstances work out. This is not to slight these ways of guidance. All we are disagreeing with is the complete exclusion of the human which sometimes accompanies such an outlook.

How then should we seek God's guidance? We suggest that there are five principles which issue from what the Bible teaches on the subject. We carefully call them *principles* and not *rules* to make it clear that we are not advocating techniques for guidance.

The Explicit Will of God
There are two uses of the expression *the will of God* in Christianity. One is the will of God which is explicit in Scripture

and is of general application, the other is the will of God which is not explicit in Scripture and is of individual application only.

The first principle of guidance is this: *Obey the explicit statements in Scripture which make clear what God's will is for everyone.* These are found everywhere in Scripture and are the general directions concerning how life should be lived by all.

For example, "This is the will of God, your sanctification..." (1 Thess. 4:3); "Rejoice always, pray constantly, give thanks in all circumstances; for this is the will of God in Christ Jesus for you" (1 Thess. 5:16-18); "Doing the will of God from the heart, rendering service with a good will as to the Lord and not to men" (Eph. 6:6-7); "It is God's will that by doing right you should put to silence the ignorance of foolish men" (1 Pet. 2:15); "Therefore do not be foolish, but understand what the will of the Lord is" (Eph. 5:17). This last exhortation follows a detailed description of the unfruitful works of darkness and the command to take no part in them, but rather to "walk as children of light." The appropriate fruit of such a life is "all that is good and right and true" (Eph. 5:9). In other words, God's will is not secret. It is explained clearly for all to read and understand.

The point is that we already have been given guidance by God for the major part of our lives. True, we are not told whether to live in one city as over against another, or to marry A and not B. These decisions of where to live and what to do are indeed of overarching significance, since they constitute the environment within which the explicit statements concerning the will of God have to be understood and obeyed. Each of us has a different life-situation. But the differences must not be exaggerated. The similarities of experience are greater than the dissimilarities: all believers have to struggle with sin, all need to walk by faith, all will be tempted. Therefore, the information given by the Bible as the will of God is guidance sufficient for the major part of of our lives. Ignorance of God's secret will is kept in proportion, balanced by God's clear, general instructions which apply regardless of our particular environment.

This first principle is important, for God guides us concerning his secret will only as we obey his explicit will. We do not live in the materialist's universe. God does exist and rewards those who seek him (Heb. 11:6). He is able to work into our experience. He is separated from us not because we are small, but because we are sinful. Once sin is dealt with "by grace through faith," the separation is ended, our lives are open to God. This concept of our openness to God must be maintained at all costs, living as we do in a post-Enlightenment, and therefore a skeptical, society. God is not dead. He is not shut out of our world. He *is* able to work into our experience in this particular moment of history and direct us. Therefore to obey God's explicit will is not futile, for he has promised to honor such obedience.

Our being open to God is the framework within which the second principle operates. As we aim to do God's explicit will, we can be sure that *he will not allow us to "get lost,"* but will keep and guide us through the bogs and thickets of life. It is not just a matter of the individual struggling to find the right path within a maze of alternatives. God himself has promised to "make straight your paths" (Prov. 3:6).

The conditions which accompany such promises, however, are equally clear: "In all your ways acknowledge him" (Prov. 3:6). "He who looks into the perfect law . . . and perseveres, being no hearer that forgets but a doer that acts, he shall be blessed in his doing" (Jas. 1:25). "Blessed is the man who walks not in the counsel of the wicked. . . . In all that he does, he prospers" (Ps. 1:1-3). God guides those who keep his explicit will.

That these promises have conditions does not mean that a believer has to be able to say, "I have kept God's will perfectly" before God will lead. If we confess our sin, turn from it and cling to Christ's work as our sole ground for confidence before God, then even though we may look back on many things which are wrong in our lives, we can rest assured God will not fail us. "Those who wait for me shall not be put to shame" (Is. 49:23). Things may seem hopeless, we may feel sinful and confused, but God will not let us go astray.

Furthermore, this principle delivers us from passivity. Often Christians are becalmed when they are uncertain about what to do in the future. They act as if there is nothing they can do, as if it is God who must do it all. This attitude is wrong. Even if we do not know what the right step should be and even if we are confused as a result, we are not confined to passivity. We have "traction," in that we know God's explicit will. Keeping that is our first priority; therefore we need continually to respect the guidance God already has given.

No Faith, No Guidance

In order not to underestimate the difficulty involved in all this we must remember the third principle—*without faith guidance is impossible*. Faith is simply *trust*. Though faith involves trusting what is unseen, it is not irrational, any more, let us say, than trusting in the existence of a train engineer is irrational because we do not see him. We have good reason to suppose that he is objectively present and reliable, and when we step on the train we put our trust in him. So with faith in God: we have objective reasons for the conviction that he exists; then we put our trust in him. That is faith within the biblical world view.

In the context of guidance, however, we want to use the phrase *battle faith*. We are not implying by this that faith changes its meaning at a certain point. *Battle faith* is faith exercised in a battle situation. Believers literally are caught up in a battle. Just as soldiers, who cannot see all the details of the battle or why certain commands are given or why relief has not arrived, nevertheless put their confidence in the commanding officer, so believers, warring against the world, the flesh and the devil, trust God even though they may not understand what is happening at a given moment.

Such faith is not automatic. It is a command and could

have been dealt with as an aspect of the first principle, for it is a part of the explicit will of God. No direction in the Bible is more common than "have faith in God." It is God's will that we should trust him. And faith in God is appropriate because he is our Savior. He already has delivered us and made us his children by adoption. We are the "apple of his eye" (Deut. 32:10; Ps. 17:8; Zech. 2:8). He has promised never to let us fall, and will never break his promise. Therefore, it is fitting that we should love him and trust him.

Moreover, faith is *necessary*. The writer to the Hebrews says, "Without faith it is impossible to please him" (Heb. 11:6), and he then gives examples from the Old Testament of those who, with battle faith, did please God. Abraham, for example, went out not knowing where he was going, and Moses who "endured as seeing him who is invisible" (Heb. 11:27), and so on. Was their response of trust within the battle irrelevant? Certainly not. The Bible says that they were established by God *because* they had faith. Faith was the means of their victory: "Through faith [they] conquered kingdoms, enforced justice, received promises, stopped the mouths of lions . . . won strength out of weakness" (Heb. 11:33-34). "This is the victory that overcomes the world, our faith" (1 Jn. 5:4).

Finally, faith is important because on occasions within the battle it seems as if there is nothing else we can do. We feel helpless, and crushed as Paul did when he said, "We were so utterly, unbearably crushed that we despaired even of life itself" (2 Cor. 1:8). We feel we cannot keep God's commandments even though we know them. We are confused and dispirited.

Sometimes this happens when the future is unclear. The insecurity of the situation, the uncertainty as to what we should do and a sense of our own unworthiness can be manipulated by the devil to cause us to feel quite lost. God may even seem to have removed himself from us as if he no longer loves us. At such times, like a child in distress, we must cry out to our heavenly Father, "Out of the depths I cry to thee,

O LORD! Lord, hear my voice!" (Ps. 130:1).

There is only one thing to do and that is to trust God. This is such a simple step. Faith does not require great emotions or energy. Jesus described it as a grain of mustard seed—a very small thing (Mt. 17:20). It may appear so small in fact that it seems like nothing to us in the moment we turn to God and cast ourselves on him. But it is not nothing; it is the means whereby mountains are removed and we are lifted up out of the miry pit.

Decide for Yourself
Faith must not be equated with passivity. This fourth principle carries us back to the discussion of sovereignty and responsibility. We want to stress that decision making is a valid part of guidance. The fact that there is no outstanding indication of God's leading, through visions or dreams or circumstances, does not mean that no action is possible. With a proper attitude toward God, we may choose for ourselves and need not fear that we are infringing on God's authority.

We do not mean to imply by this that God cannot lead through extraordinary means. An angel appeared to Mary. Joseph was shown what to do in a dream. It is a very wonderful thing to look to God out of a sense of complete helplessness and see him coming to the rescue in some remarkable way. It is this that makes the psalmist cry out, "I love the LORD, because he has heard my voice" (Ps. 116:1). By stressing that decision making is valid we are not depreciating those forms of guidance which are evidently supernatural.

Nor are we saying that the believer should hurry to make decisions. Sometimes decisions have to be made in a hurry. But in general there should be an openness to the possibility that God will act in some objective way to make his will clear. Therefore there should be a "waiting upon the Lord," that is, literally waiting for God to act. This is very important, especially as the church in the West has been so influenced by the emphasis today on efficiency, and quick solutions. When the pressures are on us, we become like the people of Israel who did not believe that God would lead them and keep them safe. Like them, we think we know better than God and hastily press on with our own ideas.

So activism is not the answer; nor is passivity. We should feel free to go ahead and make decisions, yet at the same time be careful not to lose the mentality of "waiting upon the Lord." We stress the first now because we are considering the humanness of spiritual experience and because making one's own decisions has been challenged by some teaching on the Christian life. Both sides need to be stressed, but the Bible makes it clear that our tendency is not to wait on God. Therefore we must be extremely careful that we do not simply rely on our own understanding (Ps. 146).

It is obvious from the New Testament, however, that decision making is a valid aspect of guidance. For example, in Acts 15:22 we read, "It seemed good to the apostles and elders, with the whole church, to choose men from among them and send them to Antioch." Presumably, the right course of action had been discussed in assembly and then, after careful thought and prayer, a decision had been reached. Other examples of decisions occur in Acts 19:21, 20:16; Titus 3:12; in Acts 15:36, Col. 4:7-8, 1 Thessalonians 3:1 decisions are implied. There is no conflict in these passages between the decision making of the persons involved and the leading of the Holy Spirit.

What, then, is the right way to make decisions? First, decisions have to be made prayerfully. Where time allows, all aspects of a decision should be brought before God, seeking his direction.

Second, we should ask, "Am I willing to go in a direction that I do not like or that I have not yet considered?" If we are asking God to lead us, we must be sure we are willing to be led. And "Am I trusting God?" Without becoming morbidly introspective, we must ask these two questions about our attitude. In this life, we never shall be perfectly willing nor perfectly trusting, but we must seek to be honest before God.

Third, if the circumstances allow, we should try to wait. Issues are often unclear at the beginning and time helps to clarify them. Sometimes we do not know about alternative possibilities until we have made a number of inquiries; or perhaps we have not had sufficient time to sort out our own motives. Most important of all, time gives God an opportunity to act into the situation so that we have no doubt about his will.

Many Ways of Guidance

The fifth principle is that *God guides his people in a variety of ways*. We have shown already that decision making is *one* way, but it is not the only way.

In Acts 1:15-26 the brethren used the casting of lots as a means of guidance. To suggest, as some do, that they were wrong or unspiritual to do this is dangerous for nothing in the text casts doubt on the validity of their doing this. In Acts 16:9, Paul was guided by a vision. In Acts 13:2 we read, "While they were worshiping the Lord and fasting, the Holy Spirit said, 'Set apart for me Barnabas and Saul for the work to which I have called them.'" We are not told the details, but evidently some special leading of the Spirit was involved. These are just a few examples of the variety of ways God used to guide his people during the early years of the church's existence. We must insist on the possibility of an equal variety today.

Throughout this chapter we have stressed that there is a supernatural dimension to all guidance, that guidance may take the form of extraordinary phenomena, such as visions, dreams or a remarkable conjunction of circumstances, and yet that guidance may be supernatural without being extraordinary: our decisions are as legitimate a means of guidance as any other, for God always deals with us as persons.

We are not suggesting that decision making needs to be emphasized more than other aspects. Much depends on where each individual is coming from. Some traditions within the church have neglected the extraordinary means which God sometimes uses to lead his people. Someone raised in such a tradition needs to be encouraged to "wait upon the Lord" in a way that may be quite unfamiliar. There has been an opposite tendency in much evangelical teaching, which is why we have stressed decision making. Too often Christians have been made to feel that *deciding* to do something is unspiritual, that they should rather pray and have God show them what to do in a dramatic way. But this is unnecessary. God *may* do this. Such a possibility should never be excluded. But he made us with the ability to decide and he expects us to use that ability in a godly way and for godly ends.

THE FAMILY

NINE

There has always been a curious romanticism about family life. People seem to think that simply because there is "the family" their relationships within it will automatically be good. But this is obviously untrue, for all families, composed as they are of sinners—and only sinners—are arenas for battle.

It was for this reason that Luther described family life as "the school for character."[1] He had been raised in the Roman Catholic church with the monastic ideal that one's sinful nature needed to be schooled within the secluded environment of a monastery with a strict and well-ordered regime for body and soul. When he married, he discovered there was a far more exacting, and at the same time more satisfying, school for character. Within the normal demands of the home, his sinfulness was more easily exposed and he learned what spiritual experience really was.

To draw attention to the difficulties of family life does not imply a defect in marriage. We hope in fact to uncover some of its real wonder in this chapter. But any such discussion, particularly today, must start with a realistic assessment of the difficulties, for in the West there has been a complete change in attitude toward marriage. Where previously marriage was viewed as an institution "ordained by God," now it is simply either a successful or unsuccessful contractual arrangement. Therefore, the grounds for defending the Christian view of marriage must be clear; we must never say that marriage is easy or that it guarantees happiness.

Many factors in modern society (for example, the increase of affluence and mobility, and the feminist consciousness) have strained the traditional concept of one man, one woman "till death do us part." But the principal strain has come from the changed world view of Western society—the naturalistic or materialistic revolution in philosophy which we discussed in chapter seven. Humans, it is now claimed, are simply an extension of the animal kingdom. Our habit of being faithful has no religious basis or sanction; it is simply the result of economic and personal pressures.[2] If justification for this habit has to be found anywhere it must be in the pair-bonding practice of some animal and bird species—in the field of ethology, not theology. This philosophical revolution has resulted in a completely new consensus in our society which is reflected in recent changes in laws relating to sex and marriage: divorce is now more easily obtained, abortion and homosexuality are legal.[3]

Therefore, a defense of the biblical view of marriage must not be naive. We cannot afford to be unrealistic about marriage, nor can we afford to be mere traditionalists. It is imperative that we understand what the Bible says about marriage and the family and that we defend it on that basis alone.

The Starting Point Is Creation

Once again the starting point is creation.[4] "Man" was created "male and female" (Gen. 1:27). This is the basis for the

Christian understanding of marriage. Furthermore, as "man" was created male and female with the command to produce children, our understanding of family life begins here too. Genesis 2:24 makes it clear in turn that when a child reaches adulthood he "leaves his father and mother and cleaves to his wife," thus forming a new family unit.

Genesis 1 also indicates that the family was designed to be the clearest demonstration of what is meant by the expression *the image of God.* Here we need to be careful. Each individual man and woman is the image of God in that each is a person (see chapter one). But God's personality cannot be considered apart from his diversity; three persons constitute the one true God. God is not like someone cast up on a desert island, unable to communicate with anyone. The personness of God (that God loves, for example) is fulfilled within the relationship of the members of the Trinity. Similarly, the personness of humans is fulfilled within a social experience. We may even say, therefore, that a person is the image of God *only* in community, though this does not contradict what has already been said about each individual being the image of God. A human is fulfilled not primarily as an individual alone, but rather in relationship with others.

So Genesis 1 teaches us, first, that "marriage" constitutes the original form of human relationship—not two Adams only or two Eves. Second, it teaches us that this relationship constitutes the original expression of the image of God.

This does not mean that the single person cannot be fulfilled. Because sexual intercourse is not the essence of our being (though sexuality is an integral part of our humanness) and because we were created for an experience of relationship beyond the limits of just one family (consider Jesus' command to "love your neighbor as yourself"), it is both feasible and legitimate to remain unmarried. The single person is not necessarily less fulfilled as a person just because singleness is not the norm of human experience.[5]

What we are suggesting, however, is that the relationship

of marriage—which is in fact the norm in human society —was designed by God to be the clearest demonstration and reflection of the unity and diversity experienced within the Trinity. Hence, the expression *they become one flesh* (Gen. 2:24) means not just a physical union, though obviously it includes this. Rather, it highlights an experience of unity which is possible uniquely in the exclusive and total commitment of marriage. This makes it unlike any other relationship. Becoming one flesh comprises a commitment to love within the sphere of all that makes us human, to share the whole of one's life. It includes physical union in intercourse and the amazing possibility of creating other persons with whom to share the relationship of oneness. These children are also "bone of my bones and flesh of my flesh" to each of the parents. In other words, the family is uniquely the image of God.

It is not that there are no other relationships in society which have this same character. All human relationships are relationships between persons. Therefore their glory is that they are relationships of love. This is the glory of marriage and it is the glory of friendships outside marriage as well. Though potentially there is a different order of oneness within the family than is possible between friends or within the church or society at large, all human relationships were designed to reflect God's unity within diversity.

This does not mean that all relationships have to be equal or entail the same degree of unity. The Bible gives many illustrations of friendship outside marriage: David and Jonathan, Naomi and Ruth, and Jesus and John, "the beloved disciple." There are many common elements between friendship and marriage. Friends, for example, are able to share their lives, to be loyal to one another, to have deep affinity. But friends are not committed to a lifelong relationship by divine command in the way a married couple is (normally death alone may separate them), nor is it a sexual relationship. Within the church too there is to be this oneness. Jesus said, "I am praying . . . for those whom thou hast given me ... that they may be one, even as we are one" (Jn. 17:9, 11).

The difference between marriage and relationships between friends or within the church or society is a difference of kind, not of superior/inferior. Just as animals of a particular family, say the cat family, are all equally members of that family (one species is not better than another) and yet each is distinct, so the oneness experienced within marriage is unique though the oneness experienced outside marriage is not inferior. It is simply of a different order.

The New Testament endorses this view of the uniqueness of marriage. Speaking about the proper relationship within marriage in Ephesians 5:22-33, Paul outlines the respective duties of husband and wife. The husband, he explains, is to love his wife "as Christ loved the church and gave himself up for her" (5:25). (This verse, incidentally, should be considered carefully by those who argue that Paul had a low estimate of women or a low estimate of marriage, or both.) Having drawn a parallel between marriage and Christ's relationship with the church, he quotes Genesis 2:24: "For this reason a man shall leave his father and mother and be joined to his wife, and the two shall become one flesh" (5:31) and adds this remarkable commentary: "This mystery is a profound one, and I am saying that it refers to Christ and the church" (5:32).

Paul is not by-passing marriage in saying this. He is not saying, "Marriage is of little importance; the important thing is Christ's relationship with the church." On the contrary, he is concerned to establish right relationships within marriage.

His use of the word *mustērion* ("mystery") is interesting. Normally he uses it to refer to a truth which we cannot discover for ourselves but is kept secret, "a mystery," until God chooses to make it known (see, for example, Eph. 3:4-5). Such a meaning in the marriage context, however, is unlikely. Why then does Paul choose this particular term? We suggest that it is because marriage is revelatory, that it reveals something about our relationship with God. On other occasions when he uses *mustērion,* he is thinking of something being revealed *in words* about the meaning of Christ's work of salvation. Here, something is being revealed not in words but *through an aspect of creation,* through marriage. The proper relationship between husband and wife typifies the relationship between Christ and the church. This is why marriage is a mystery.

Within the same letter, however, he extends the idea beyond the relationship of husband and wife to include the family. He says, "I bow my knees before the Father, from whom every family in heaven and on earth is named" (Eph. 3:14-15). The infinite, living God has made finite persons in his likeness and their experience within families resembles the experience within the Trinity. Far from humans projecting a "father figure" into the heavens (because of our sense of weakness within the universe), God, the Father, has made us like himself. Humans are able to experience unity and diversity within marriage and so marriage testifies to God's own unity and diversity. So also we are able to experience human fatherhood because "fatherhood" is first found in the Trinity.

The basis for the Christian view of the family is found in creation. This is yet another area of spiritual experience which is illuminated by the organizing principle stated in chapter one. The family considered as the fullest expression of the image of God is not simply a theoretical idea. It starts the whole consideration of the family where it should be started—in the recovery of our original identity which, in this case, means the restoration of the family to its intended character. At the beginning, the family was intended to demonstrate most completely the relationships within the Trinity, and to be the unit within which we would enjoy most completely the kind of relationships enjoyed within the Trinity. Can a more noble foundation for marriage and the family be conceived? This is the heart of the Christian view of the family.

Authority Is Not the Answer

Recently, there has been a veritable flood of Christian books on marriage and the family. Unfortunately, most of them fail to carry the discussion back to creation and consequently they present a very restricted view of the family. We are not saying that these books have no value because of this omission, or even that there is not considerable value in some.

There are two principal dangers. The first is the tendency to make authority the central issue and the source of all true enjoyment in family life. The second is a closely related and equally imbalanced emphasis on techniques as the solution to lack of structure in family life. We have discussed this already in other contexts and the problem is much the same in reference to marriage. By labeling emphasis on authority a *danger,* we are not suggesting that authority is unimportant within the family. It has been neglected in modern society, resulting in terrible confusion and sorrow, and needs to be emphasized today. Also, a structure has been laid down in God's Word—husbands are over wives and parents are over children—and it is vital to hold onto this firmly. But we insist that authority is not the focal point in a consideration of marriage and the family.

Equally it is a danger to overemphasize techniques. Some Christians, while rightly advocating discipline, have spelled out the methods of discipline in minute detail. This is a serious mistake. Though following someone's rules for a happy family seems easy and often appears to "work" (because people generally function better with structure than without it), there is a terrible danger of legalism. And nothing can be uglier in family relationships than such legalism. It creates inflexibility in the parents and resentment in the children simply because the rules "must" be observed at all costs.

Of course discussion of techniques can be desirable: one family can say to another, "Arranging our family life like this has made a difference to us all" and the suggestion may in fact prove helpful. But the recent emphasis on techniques so concentrates on means that the end is lost sight of. The model of the family becomes mechanical, rather than personal. The criterion for success becomes "How efficiently do we conform to a certain authority's suggested techniques for having a happy family?" rather than "Do we really love each other?"

This is terribly important in a fallen world, for having the right starting point is not just a theoretical issue: starting from creation yields a very different outcome in practice than do the approaches which center on either authority or techniques or a combination of the two. For example, when we understand that the family is to reflect the relationship between the members of the Trinity, we realize that diversity is not a problem: diversity does not necessarily work against unity in a family any more than it does among the Father, the Son and the Holy Spirit. This is true of all types of diversity, whether of personality, gifts, interests, structures in the home or other areas. We should not expect each family to operate in the same way nor expect any one family to operate always in the same way. We should learn to accept and encourage diversity where the differences are not contrary to what God has commanded in the Bible. (Polygamy, for example, is an infringement whereas interracial marriage is not.) Only the laws of God are of universal application.

All other techniques of how to organize family life must be viewed critically. There is no particular virtue attached to conforming to a certain fashion in child-rearing (for example, how to toilet train) or adhering to a timetable or stressing tidiness, because each family is different. One family can tolerate a low level of tidiness which makes another scream. One couple can go to bed late while another must go to bed early. For one child a certain type of discipline may be helpful while for another it may be harmful. It is foolish and perverse to expect uniformity in such areas.

If we Christians had realized this and included it in our teaching, we could have encouraged humanness instead of

working against it. We could have challenged the inflexibility of the conformist approach in the family as much as in society. Instead, we have often espoused conformity, mistaking it for righteousness. This is the greatest danger in some of the books which Christians have written recently on family life. By their concentration on techniques (good as some of these may be), they encourage a conformist approach and hence an attitude which is incompatible with the Christian faith. Grace, diversity and humanness are lost; legalism, conformism and the inhumanity of mechanical structures begin to prevail.

We are repudiating neither authority nor rules of human origin. Each family must have some rules in order to exist, for example, times of meals or times at which children go to bed. In these areas obedience is proper and essential. Having a framework liberates a family; children who come to accept these sorts of rules as a part of life are much happier for it. Parents and children alike need a framework. The fact that the rules are *human,* not divine, should never be forgotten, but this makes no difference concerning obedience. Both parents and children should respect and obey whatever rules apply to them.

Though since the Fall authority has been essential (just as it is essential in government) and human rules are necessary, neither of these must be treated as central. Unfortunately, it is so easy for this to happen. There is a utopian streak in us all: we have a picture in our minds of what love and unity in the home should mean, of a well-organized, frictionless, smoothly flowing existence. But when we look at the reality, it discourages us. There seems to be such a high level of confusion—babies crying, sickness, quarrels, unexpected guests, conflicting commitments and so on. This is the way life is—very unutopian, full of loose ends.

Life is also complex. Dealing with children at different ages and therefore with different needs, having to adjust to no two weeks being exactly the same, each person having problems which change from day to day, tiredness, special temptation, sorrow because of death in the family, or difficulties at school are just a few examples of complication. Life is never simple. This complexity is further tangled up because of sin. Family members are sinful people, not machines—the parents as much as the children. How then can there *ever* be a smoothness and neatness of life, particularly if (as *should* be the case) the family is also living not just for itself but for others as well—trying to be hospitable, looking after aged parents or relations, bearing the burdens of those around them?

By emphasizing diversity and variety, we are trying to push beyond relative, human approaches to family life to God's original intention in creating marriage and the family. The model of the family is *not* that of an efficiently run business. To introduce such a model is to destroy the very possibility of humanness in the family. This is why we lean against the authority/techniques approach. Family life is always full of loose ends. That does not mean that family life should be completely confused. Just as the church is directed to do all things "decently and in order," so the family must work toward order.

The result of the utopian approach to order in the home, however, is perpetual frustration. One expects a degree of order which is unattainable, for life is abnormal and the family is no exception. In fact, the family exposes the abnormality as much as anything in society. Consequently, life becomes unbearable for the person who thinks, "If I do such-and-such, then all the frustrations and confusions of family life will be remedied and we shall live happily ever after." Concentrating on techniques may achieve a more efficiently run organization *called* the family. But it will never develop a living organism which *is* a family revealing God's character and person.

In the family, the focal point must be the Trinity. Because each member of the Trinity loves, the fact that each member is distinct does not deprive the relationship of unity. Love "binds everything together in perfect harmony" (Col.

3:14). In the same way the members of a family are to love one another, and rejoice in their diversity. They will maintain the principle of authority because it is necessary, just as the Law is necessary to show us how we ought to live. Though they may apply techniques because they are helpful, they will avoid a mentality which focuses on authority and rules.

Having discussed the proper basis for the family (rejecting authority and techniques as the central focus of family life), let us now turn to consider the proper exercise of authority within the family.

Authority—a Means, Not an End

In the biblical view, authority is not an end but a means to an end. It is necessary because it enables society to function. In the area of government, rulers are to be respected and obeyed. But such authority is simply a framework for the normal affairs that constitute human experience. The important thing is not government but life. Government exists only in order that life may function and flourish. Likewise, the Bible insists on an authority structure in the home, not as an end in itself but as a necessary means to the proper enjoyment of life.

This view of authority as a means to an end together with our understanding of the proper end in family life—that the family is to reflect the image of God—leads us to two important conclusions as to how authority is to function within the family. First, authority is to function under the authority of God's Word. Second, the authority is to function within the context of mutuality.

Authority is never to be arbitrary. The distinction between God's laws and human rules must always be clear. Only God's laws are absolute. Where human rules are necessary, they must be introduced only to support the first. Where they are challenged, there must be a willingness to change. Parents must therefore examine the human rules which they have set up: Why do we do things this way? Is it simply because people did it when we were young? Is it simply because this is the fashion today? Are we just trying to give ourselves an easy time? They must struggle against the conformist approach without falling into the opposite danger of being nonconformist for its own sake. They must seek to be conformed to a way of life which God says is good.

Moreover, authority must not be exercised in an arbitrary manner. There must be a serious attempt to rule justly. Parents may be justified, for example, in punishing a certain wrongdoing, yet be too harsh in the punishment. Or they may react out of impatience or tiredness and punish unjustly. In such cases there must be a willingness to apologize. Just judgment needs no apology. "But when the wicked rule, the people groan" (Prov. 29:2).

Secondly, the goal of the exercise of authority is *mutuality*. This means that authority is to promote family relationships in which, despite the many defects of that love, the warmth of affection is clearly expressed and felt, relationships in which people say, "I love you," not out of habit but because they mean it.

The relationships must be characterized by self-giving. Paul's introduction to his discussion of the family in Ephesians 5:21—6:9 is striking. He says, "Submit to one another out of reverence for Christ" (NIV). This exhortation applies to husbands as well as to wives, to parents as well as to children, to masters as well as to servants. They are all to have the attitude of giving themselves up for the other, since that is what Christ has done for them. Paul spells this out with regard to the husband's attitude toward the wife. The husband's submission to his wife is to include giving himself up for her. That he says this without violating the authority structure of the husband over the wife is instructive in the present feminist debate. Authority does not necessarily threaten a love relationship within marriage because authority is not the focus of the relationship.

The term *mutuality* conveys the idea of togetherness, of acting together and deciding together. The central theme in the relationship is not authority. Certainly it is not superiority. Paul says the husband is to *serve* the wife. Even more basic, looking back to the creation, Adam and Eve were made equally the image of God and men and women still are equally "God's image." True, the relationship of husband and wife will reflect the authority structure, but authority should not be its principal characteristic. The principal characteristic should be that they think, pray, struggle, rear their children and do everything else *together*.

The husband and wife may act freely within the biblical framework, without subdividing their lives into *decision making* for the husband and *nondecision making* for the wife. So, too, with the issue of roles: does the mother take care of the home and children; and the father, the office and garden? Obviously, some subdivision of labor is necessary but it will come at different places for different people. The husband may do the cooking and the wife take care of the accounts. (No divine principle is thereby infringed.) What must be avoided at all costs is the idea that the *relationship* is divided because of the division of *labor*. The spouses are to be integrated in the whole range of their lives. They constitute a new entity which Scripture calls "one flesh." Their life together must reflect this. If work or a sport or a hobby is inhibiting this sort of togetherness, it must be cut off or restrained ruthlessly, though this is not to say that work or sports or hobbies are invalid. Still, their choice of activities and priorities have to be chosen seriously and maintained carefully, for in a fallen world the enjoyment of togetherness does not come automatically.

The target to be aimed at within the relationship is principally the experience of mutuality—the sharing of one another's lives expressed in an attitude of submission, of a willingness to give oneself away out of concern for the other and out of reverence for Christ. Because human beings are designed for such a relationship, it will not damage them. In fact, this is the only way to find fulfillment within marriage. The opposite ideal, seeking to keep intact one's own life, insisting on one's own rights, resenting whatever is costly to oneself in terms of time or energy, spells ruin to the couple and the family.

This is where so many of the ideas of the women's liberation movement are wrong.[6] Some of the ideas are completely right and we should support them (for example, equal pay for equal work, equal opportunity). But there is no doubt that its chief characteristic is an ideal of fulfillment for women which is essentially self-centered. We reject this not because it comes from women. The attitude is just as reprehensible on the other side—and certainly it is more common among men. Much of the emotional force among liberationists comes from the fact that men have been so selfish within marriage. Nevertheless, feminist attitudes are also the result of a general redefinition of self-fulfillment today as "what I like, when I like, how I like." The effects of this are lethal.

The Christian must insist that fulfillment in marriage is the result of an attitude of self-giving by each spouse. Mutuality means acting together, being so involved in the other's life that one is prepared to "spend and be spent" for the other. This must have pre-eminence over the authority. To reverse the order is to confuse God's intention at creation, for Adam and Eve were made for one another, to love and enjoy one another—not for the one to dominate the other.

Parents and Children
What we have said of marriage applies also to the parent/child relationship. There must be a proper regard for authority on both sides: children are to be taught to obey and they are to be helped to understand the importance of authority; parents are to accept their responsibility to rule well within the home, creating a good framework, judging justly within it and not provoking the children to anger (Eph. 6:4).

But there also must be a regard, more, *devotion* to the principle of mutuality. Parents are to seek to live together with their children and not merely to bring them up. They should always be cultivating a warm relationship by expressing their love and by respecting their children right from the beginning. They should not laugh at them as if in their simplicity of expression they were subhuman, nor talk disparagingly of them in their presence as if they were unable to understand. Parents should do enjoyable things frequently with their children, not once a year as a special treat. The relationship should be something the children enjoy in the present and one which, in retrospect, is full of happy memories—as far as is possible within an abnormal world.

This is not romanticism. It is the essence of such relationships. As in all relationships, the key is "the measure you give will be the measure you get back" (Lk. 6:38). While trying to express his desire to have a warm relationship with the Corinthians, Paul uses the analogy of the parent/child relationship: "I am ready to visit you for the third time, and I will not be a burden to you, because what I want is not your possessions but you. After all, children should not have to save up for their parents, but parents for their children. So I will very gladly spend for you everything I have and expend myself as well" (2 Cor. 12:14-15 NIV).

This is the model for mutuality in the parent/child relationship. The parents are not to think of authority and discipline as the focus of their relationship. Rather, the focus must be the willingness to share their lives with their children beyond just providing them with food, clothing, a home and education. They must be willing to share their whole selves, to spend and be spent for their children. After all, men and women spend themselves in the cause of business ventures and political campaigns. Why can parents not spend themselves for their children? Why can they not give them time, give them their lives to share, give them their physical energy? The husband is to spend himself for his wife, the wife for her husband and both are to spend themselves for their children.

Another vital element within the concept of mutuality in

the parent/child relationship, namely, the temporariness of the period of dependence, must also be borne in mind. Small children are completely dependent on their parents. During this period they need to be directed by the parents. At a certain point, however, they have to move from dependence to equality with their parents. Genesis 2:24 speaks of a man leaving his father and mother when he gets married. But this does not mean that marriage should be considered the moment of independence. The independence of the child should be a goal to which the parents aim. And it should be fostered deliberately so that with each succeeding year, quietly and perhaps imperceptibly because of its gradualness, the child moves from being under the parents to being alongside them. The Bible gives no age at which this is to be achieved, but it is clearly the whole intention of the parent/child relationship. The parents are to view themselves only as *in loco parente*, that is, in the place of the parenthood of God. This is what should be uppermost in their minds. In the sense of having their children dependent on them, they are parents for only a short period. God alone is the child's permanent parent. Therefore, they are to aim at withdrawing gradually from their position of authority.

The Bible insists that children should honor their parents always since they have derived their very existence from them, but this does not mean they have to obey their parents always. Children need never obey when commanded to do something which is against the law of God. In addition, at a certain point they must go their own way whether their parents approve or not. They have to choose what job to do, what person to marry, what town to live in. For to work out one's own life under the authority of God himself is what it means to be a human being.

So, then, the parents should see themselves gradually relinquishing their authority and actually taking steps to achieve this, so that at the earliest age, without making their children prematurely adult and depriving them of the great pleasures and freedoms of childhood, the children stand as independent individuals before God and the world. Parents are to aim, in other words, at winning their children to an acceptance of God's immediate authority over them in place of God's authority mediated to them through their parents. As this happens, they will be winning their children to friendship with themselves. Is there any reason why there cannot be friendships among the members of a single family as deep as those outside it? In our disjointed society, we have come to expect only shallowness and enmity in the family.

It is difficult to describe adequately the beauty of marriage. We have mentioned repeatedly the difficulties involved simply in order to be realistic. Nothing is further from the truth than the idea that marriage solves problems, that marriage ushers one into an experience without difficulties in which one lives happily ever after. But the difficulties arise from sin and not from the institution of marriage itself. Problems should be likened to the stages of a mountaineer's ascent—each new foothold is costly but also rewarding with the vistas it opens up. The analogy is a weak one, however, for the panoramas opened up by family experience are not so much impersonal ones which delight the eyes, as spiritual and personal ones which ravish the heart.

The creation of a family is one of the most demanding and, at the same time, one of the most fulfilling of human possibilities. It is the unit which God created originally to be his image. To whatever degree a family recovers the experience intended at creation, to that extent they can enter into the glory of God's own internal experience within the "family" of the Trinity. What a majestic foundation for marriage. What an encouragement to persevere through the difficulties, knowing that riches of experience such as these lie so close at hand.

THE BELIEVER'S JUDGMENT

TEN

Human responsibility—the determination of our eternal destiny according to whether or not we believe in Christ—establishes the principle of humanness more securely than anything else. "I have set before you life and death, blessing and curse; therefore choose life, that you and your descendents may live" (Deut. 30:19). "Why will you die, O house of Israel? For I have no pleasure in the death of any one, says the Lord GOD; so turn, and live" (Ezek. 18:31-32). It is not that our efforts can secure us the reward of heaven, of eternal life with God; only the righteousness of Christ secures this for us and our faith is simply the hand that receives his gift.

Many in our culture have denied any significance to human choice and action because they have accepted the doctrine that man lives in an uncreated universe. But Christians have confidence that everything is made by the infinite God and that, therefore, as his children, we have value and our choices and actions have eternal consequences. So we have to ask ourselves and each other, "How shall we then live? Shall we choose life or death?" Let us shake ourselves free from the ashes of our culture's departure from the sure foundation of God's Word and take hold of the life which is life indeed as we come to Christ.

We have stressed throughout this book that everything we do as humans made in God's image is important. We will not be swallowed up in God; we are not to be passive, allowing ourselves to be pressed into the mold of the world around us; we need not be paralyzed by believing that God's sovereignty crushes our freedom. Instead, we have shown that God *wants* us to use our minds; he calls us to make decisions as to how we shall serve him. But what of our service after we first believe in him? What value do our actions have? Is their significance only temporary? Do the effects of our choices endure only until death, and then fade like flowers?

We must say a resounding NO, on two counts. First, what we do as believers is the evidence of the reality of our faith. Second, there is a judgment of believers when all we have done will be tested by God and approved or rejected.

Evidence of Faith

There are many statements in the Bible about the need for our faith in Christ to be a living faith which produces life and obedience. Paul reminds the Corinthians that they cannot be lenient to sinfulness among themselves: "Do you not know that the unrighteous will not inherit the kingdom of God? Do not be deceived; neither the immoral, nor idolaters, nor adulterers, nor sexual perverts, nor thieves, nor the greedy, nor drunkards, nor revilers, nor robbers will inherit the kingdom of God" (1 Cor. 6:9-10). Paul reminds his converts that they have been washed clean from their guilt by Christ's blood, and so they must not continue in unrighteous behavior.

Jesus himself states repeatedly that there can be no empty appeal to faith, for true faith is expressed not only in words but by obedience to his commandments.

Not every one who says to me, "Lord, Lord," shall enter the kingdom of heaven, but he who does the will of my Father who is in heaven. On that day many will say to me, "Lord, Lord, did we not prophesy in your name, and cast out demons in your name, and do many mighty works in your name?" And then will I declare to them, "I never knew you; depart from me, you evildoers." (Mt. 7:21-23) James puts it very simply: "Faith by itself, if it has no works, is dead" (Jas. 2:17).

People often have said that there is a conflict between James and Paul over the relationship between faith and works. Even some modern evangelicals have said there are diverse theological positions in the New Testament and have cited this subject.[1] Perhaps the strongest statement of all, however, comes from Paul himself: "I pommel my body and subdue it, lest after preaching to others I myself should be disqualified" (1 Cor. 9:27). Paul, describing the intensity of his struggle against his sinful nature, says quite plainly that he made such a great effort lest he, having preached to others, should "fail the test" (the literal meaning of the Greek *adokimos*). Charles Hodge's comment on this passage is worth quoting at length.

What an argument and what a reproof is this! The reckless and listless Corinthians thought they could safely indulge themselves to the very verge of sin, while this devoted apostle considered himself as engaged in a life-struggle for his salvation. This same apostle, however, who evidently acted on the principle that the righteous scarcely are saved, and that the kingdom of heaven suffereth violence, at other times breaks out in the most joyful assurance of salvation, and says that he was persuaded that nothing in heaven, earth or hell could ever separate him from the love of God (Rom. 8:38, 39). The one state of mind is the necessary condition of the other. It is only those who are conscious of this constant and deadly struggle with sin, to whom this assurance is given. In the very same breath Paul says, "Oh wretched man that I am;" and "Thanks be to God who giveth us the victory" (Rom. 7:24, 25). It is the indolent and self-indulgent Christian who is always in doubt.[2]

We must be careful to avoid confusion here. As Hodge points out, Paul does not contradict his teaching about justification being only through faith in Christ when he makes this statement about himself. Also, such an emphasis on the necessity of works does not mean that the person who believes just before death cannot be saved because there is no time to show evidence of faith. The thief on the cross believed and went straight to Paradise on his death. The merit which saves us from judgment and death is Christ's, not our own. However, for those of us who live after professing faith, there is to be a demonstration in the world of the genuineness of our commitment. Our faith is not to be stillborn, like a child dead at birth; rather, the initial step of faith is to be the beginning of a life of obedience to God.

As we have stressed earlier, this necessity of obedience does not mean a refocusing of our attention away from Christ onto ourselves, so that our confidence before God's judgment throne becomes our obedience rather than Christ's righteousness. No, for the same Paul who disciplined himself so as not to be disqualified says, "That I may gain Christ and be found in him, not having a righteousness of my own, based on law, but that which is through faith in Christ, the righteousness from God that depends on faith" (Phil. 3:9).

If someone is engaged to be married, the engagement must be followed by a growing relationship and the consummation of marriage, otherwise the engagement is null and void. So for the Christian, commitment to Christ must be followed and evidenced by a turning to him day by day, serving, loving and obeying him. The everyday life of faith, then, is of eternal consequence.

Judgment
The second truth which shows that our choices and actions

as believers are not only of temporary significance is the believer's judgment. Christians are often reluctant to deal with this doctrine—for perhaps three reasons. First, there is a proper fear of drawing attention away from Christ's work as the ground of salvation and putting in its place a doctrine of purgatory or of salvation by good works. Second, the false teaching called "cheap grace"—stressing God's grace but neglecting entirely the believer's responsibility—has led to a complacent resting on Christ. Third, there has been a general downgrading of the biblical emphasis on human significance. These three together have created a silence on the subject of a judgment for the believer.

Before moving to the subject itself, let it be clear that Scripture says nothing about purgatory. By *judgment* we do not mean a punishment of the Christian by God for his wrongdoing and failures, nor a period of refinement by fire after death. No, indeed, for Hebrews says that Christ "is able for all time to save those who draw near to God through him" (7:25) and "He has appeared once for all at the end of the age to put away sin by the sacrifice of himself" (9:26). God will not impute our sins to us. Rather, he will impute to us the righteousness of Christ, so we need have no fear of condemnation (Jn. 3:18; 5:24). As those who believe in Christ, we can have confidence for the day of judgment.

By *believer's judgment* we mean an examination, a testing of all that we have done since we first believed. Paul describes it this way:

> No other foundation can any one lay than that which is laid, which is Jesus Christ. Now if anyone builds on the foundation with gold, silver, precious stones, wood, hay, straw—each man's work will become manifest; for the Day will disclose it, because it will be revealed with fire, and the fire will test what sort of work each one has done. If the work which any man has built on the foundation survives, he will receive a reward. If any man's work is burned up, he will suffer loss, though he himself will be saved, but only as through fire. (1 Cor. 3:11-15)

Paul is discussing his work as an apostle in the context of this passage but it is clear that what he says applies to all believers. Elsewhere, the New Testament refers to the same testing in the context of, for example, leaders in the church (Heb. 13:17) and masters and servants (Col. 3:22—4:1).

Everything that we do as believers will be tested by God. The worthlessness of that which is sinful and without value—like hay, straw or wood—will be exposed and destroyed by the fire of God's searching examination. We will not be condemned because of the worthless things we have built; rather, we shall be saved because of Christ in spite of our failures. But we will experience the loss of all that was wrong, all that was done with false motivation. Christ says that if we do things in order to be seen and approved by others, then we will have had all the reward we will ever get; God will give us no further reward (Mt. 6:1-6).

We will experience loss in the sense that we will see clearly, as God sees, just what we have done and why we have done it. We will see the good and the bad, and the bad will be consumed by fire. It will not accrue to our condemnation, for Christ always lives to make intercession for those who have trusted in him (Heb. 7:25). God in his mercy will approve and reward what is good; the gold, silver and precious stones will survive the fire.

We must not shrink back from stressing this for fear of slighting Christ's work. This is no slight to Christ, for sin is so pervasive in our lives that God would be unable to accept anything we have done were it not for Christ covering our guilt. We are like an apple which has brown spots right through to its core. It is impossible to separate the good from the bad so we have to throw the apple away. But God does not throw us away. He accepts us in the Beloved and can separate the rottenness from the good—that is the believer's judgment. In his love God approves the good that remains, for it is presented to him on the foundation of Christ. When our children present us with the first birthday card they have made, in love we overlook the imperfections, the hurried work, the smudges and mistakes and see, rather, the offering of love. So it is with God. He will see clearly the blemishes in our lives but the love he has expressed in Christ will mean that he will approve what is good.

Thus, we find many statements in the New Testament about this subject. Jesus says, "Nothing is covered up that will not be revealed, or hidden that will not be known. Therefore whatever you have said in the dark shall be heard in the light, and what you have whispered in private rooms shall be proclaimed upon the housetops" (Lk. 12:2-3); and "Lay up for yourselves treasure in heaven" (Mt. 6:20). Paul commands the rich "to do good, to be rich in good deeds, liberal and generous, thus laying up for themselves a good foundation for the future" (1 Tim. 6:18-19). "What is our hope or joy or crown of boasting before our Lord Jesus at his coming? Is it not you? For you are our glory and joy" (1 Thess. 2:19-20). "In the day of Christ I may be proud that I did not run in vain or labor in vain" (Phil. 2:16). These are but a few of the many Scriptures stressing the importance of what we do now for the day of judgment.

Hope and Joy and Crown
What do all these references mean? Paul's metaphor of a building which we erect on the foundation of Christ is not superficial. We are building things in our lives which will literally last forever. We may agree with Shakespeare that "the evil that men do lives after them," but the good is not interred with their bones. We easily forget the good others have done but God remembers all, and all will be revealed: the secrets of every heart, each cup of cold water given to someone thirsty, every hand reached out to someone falling, every word of encouragement to one lonely and downcast, every effort to proclaim the gospel to those around us, every visit to the sick or imprisoned, every penny that has been given with a cheerful heart.

God will reveal all these and he will reward them. What will the reward be? We can say at the least that Scripture suggests two things. First, there will be the approval of God himself: "As you did it to one of the least of these my brethren, you did it to me" (Mt. 25:40). Second, there will be the joy for us of seeing the effects of our actions. It is this which Paul means when he writes of his "joy or crown of boasting" (1 Thess. 2:19). There will be the enjoyment of seeing the results of the good works that were built on the foundation of Christ. We should understand this quite literally. Paul says that he will see those he has helped through his ministry. So, if we have, for example, given money to someone in need, we will see the effects of that gift. If we have supported others by giving or prayer, we will see the effects of what we have done and enjoy the fruits. All of us are making ripples in the waters of life which go on forever. Very often we know little about those ripples, but God will manifest them to us and approve what is good.

As we see what we have done, we will realize more clearly than ever before how all flowed out of the grace of Christ to us in saving us, giving us new life, empowering us, forgiving and helping us, and not giving us our deserts but surrounding us with his love. As Paul says, "I worked harder than any of them, though it was not I, but the grace of God which is with me" (1 Cor. 15:10). Like the elders before the throne we will cast down our crowns before the Lord and praise him for his power and goodness to us (Rev. 4:10). God will give us crowns of commendation and reward but we shall give them back to him. After all he has done for us, we have been unprofitable servants (Lk. 17:10) when we consider what we ought to have done. Emphasizing the believer's judgment, therefore, does not detract from Christ. It should rather be another ground for exalting him, for then we will see his grace to us perfectly and praise him perfectly for the first time in our lives.

This life can be likened to a musical prelude; eternity in the presence of the Lord will be the body of the music. We are to begin themes now which will be played out and elaborated forever. Relationships are begun now which will be consummated and enjoyed; help given to a stranger will be returned a hundredfold.

This underlines the principle of humanness in the most striking way. Since everything we do has eternal consequences, how significant all our choices and actions are. This is true for all humanity, believers and unbelievers. While the believer is laying up a harvest of righteousness, the unbeliever is laying up a harvest of unrighteousness which will not be covered by the work of Christ. Each sin with all its consequences will be exposed by God and will be condemned—without mercy—for there was a refusal to acknowledge the wrong and turn to Christ for mercy. The true horror of all one's wrongdoing will be manifested as James says:

> Come now, you rich, weep and howl for the miseries that are coming upon you. Your riches have rotted and your garments are moth-eaten. Your gold and silver have rusted, and their rust will be evidence against you and will eat your flesh like fire. You have laid up treasure for the last days. Behold, the wages of the laborers who mowed your fields, which you kept back by fraud, cry out; and the cries of the harvesters have reached the ears of the Lord of hosts. You have lived on the earth in luxury and in pleasure; you have fattened your hearts in a day of slaughter. (Jas. 5:1-5)

Personal experience will continue for all humankind. For the believer in Christ there will be the joy of seeing Christ face to face, and the enjoyment of all the relationships which he has begun in the present with no sorrow of separation clouding them. For the unbeliever only a harvest of corruption and bitterness will remain.

God himself sets such store on our humanness that our future forever rests upon our choice. Also he will examine all that we have done and judge it. Let *us* not set less store on our lives.

God has made us in his image, and he has called us to love him and keep his commandments. Such love and obedience is not insignificant to him, however small it may seem in our own eyes. All is meaningful and all is to be weighed. "For we must all appear before the judgment seat of Christ, so that each one may receive good or evil, according to what he has done in the body" (2 Cor. 5:10). Since God has adopted us in Christ as his beloved children, let us yield up every moment of our days to his service as those who will have to give an account of ourselves to him.

FAITH/SCIENCE 197

MANY VIEWS 12

MORAL RELATIVISM 199, 19

CHOICES 32

EVIDENS 33

EVANGELISM 34

MAN AS MACHINE 36

CALLING 38

CREATOR/CREATURE 44

LANGUAGE 45, 47, 58

SACRED/SECULAR 54

SPIRITUALITY 55

SUMMARY 61

TWO FALSE PATHS 62F

MIND 79

LAW 98, 205

CHANGE 98F

Perfection 100

Presenting Gospel 107

Reasonable 108

Choice 110

Possessions 120

CENTER-OF-GRAVITY 122F

MATERIALISM 127

CONVERSION 128

NEEDY 132

Negatives of Scripture 136

TRUTH 139

EVANGELISM 143F

WHOLE COUNSEL OF God 153

SINGLES 171 & F.n.6

Friends 172

mystery 173f

NOTES

Chapter 1

[1]Two things need to be said about our attitude toward the Bible. First, *this view of the Bible is the traditional view held by the church.* It was the view of the early church, of the Reformation, of Protestantism as a whole until near the end of the nineteenth century in America (and slightly earlier in England), and of the Roman Catholic church until the encyclical "Divino afflante Spiritu" (1943). (In the case of the Roman Catholic church, however, the authority of Scripture was totally prejudiced by the authority attached to the magisterium of the church.) The attitude to the Bible was uniform: it not only "contained" the Word of God, but was the Word of God written. The terms *infallible* and *inerrant* have been used to emphasize this. Within the current debate on Scripture it is important to add that by these terms we mean that the Bible is without error, not only in its theological statements (for example, God is a God of love, or God desires to save humankind, or salvation is in Christ), but also in its statements about history and science. Modern liberal Catholicism (though this was the accepted view of the Vatican II Council also) and some of those who are called new evangelicals have introduced the same dichotomy between faith and science which was first introduced by Schleiermacher near the end of the eighteenth century. On the new evangelicals, see note on Rogers, p. 208 n. 19. On Vatican II, note Hans Küng's summary statement on the day the Vatican II Council ended (Sunday Times, Dec. 12, 1965, p. 11): "In the face of all the conservative attacks ... the historical critical method has received explicit

approval. Scripture is claimed to be inerrant only for religious truths and not for statements of a scientific or historical nature." On the traditional view of Scripture see Calvin, *Institutes* III.2.6: "So long as your mind entertains any misgivings as to the certainty of the Word, its authority will be weak and dubious, or rather it will have no authority at all. Nor is it sufficient to believe that God is true and cannot lie or deceive, unless you feel firmly persuaded that every word which proceeds from him is sacred, inviolable Truth." See also C. J. Costello's comment on Augustine of Hippo quoted by J. W. Montgomery in *Crisis in Lutheran Theology* (Grand Rapids: Zondervan, 1967): "There is no point of doctrine more plainly asserted or more vigorously defended by Augustine than the absence of falsehood and error from the divine Scriptures. . . . Indeed inerrancy is so intimately bound up with inspiration that an inspired book cannot assert what is not true. . . . It is impossible for Scripture to contain contradictory statements. One book of the Bible cannot contradict another, nor can the same author contradict himself." And in his *Commentary on the Whole Bible,* Joseph Benson said: "In such an age and nation as this [Britain 1815] to say anything in commendation of the Scriptures seems perfectly unnecessary; their truth, excellency and utility being acknowledged by high and low, rich and poor, from one end of the land to the other" (London: Wesleyan Conference Office, 1930, Vol. 1, p. 1). Finally, Kirsop Lake, "How many were there, for instance in Christian churches in the 18th century who doubted the infallible inspiration of all Scripture? A few perhaps, but very few. No, the fundamentalist may be wrong; I think that he is. But it is we [that is, liberals] who have departed from the tradition, not he. . . . The Bible and the Corpus Theologicum of the church is on the fundamentalist side" (*The Religion of Yesterday and Tomorrow,* p. 61; pub. unknown).

Second, *to consider that the Bible is true (as discussed above) does not involve a blind submission to religious authority.* The Bible is indeed our authority in all that has been said, but it is an authority we have accepted because it commends itself as being objectively true. See F. A. Schaeffer, *The God Who Is There* (Downers Grove: InterVarsity Press, 1968), pp. 92ff. The value of Schaeffer's argument is precisely that it is an application of the argument expressed by Paul in Romans 1:18ff. in which Paul argues that the truth about God is obvious, and that therefore man in rejecting it, is being a fool. See also our discussion on the mind in chap. seven.

[2]See our note on anti-intellectualism, chap. seven, f.n. eleven.

[3]Compare John Calvin, *Commentary on Genesis* (London: Banner of Truth Trust, 1975), p. 296. Concerning Genesis 9:6 he says, "Should any one object that this divine image has been obliterated, the solution is easy; first, there yet exists some remnant of it so that man is possessed of no small dignity; and, secondly, the celestial Creator himself, however corrupted man may be, still keeps in view the end of his original creation; and according to his example, we ought to consider for what end he created men, and what excellence he has bestowed upon them

above the rest of living things."

[4]H. J. Blackham, *Objections to Humanism* (London: Constable, 1963), p. 119. See also Harry Blamires, *The Christian Mind* (London: SPCK, 1963). "If you wish to meet... with the soul of modern man... turn to Beckett's novels and to his plays.... Here is a bafflement of the soul—an inner cluelessness prior to that state of organized interrogation at which one can ask: 'What is the meaning of life? What is the purpose of anything? *Here is a primitive lostness which allows for nothing so confident as a question* (for to ask a question is to presuppose a possible answer, a system of logic, a rationale at the back of things). Here one fumbles for the very means of utterance" (p. 10). And see James W. Sire, *The Universe Next Door* (Downers Grove, IL: InterVarsity Press, 1975), 99ff.

[5]On the problem of moral relativism, Aldous Huxley's *Brave New World* provides a helpful illustration. If *right* is what society decides and nothing more, then what is right today may be wrong tomorrow. This is an alarming prospect in the light of modern technological power. See F. A. Schaeffer, *How Should We Then Live?* (Old Tappan, NJ: Revell, 1976).

[6]H. S. Milford, ed., *The Complete Works of William Cowper* (Oxford: Oxford University Press, 1913), p. 217, lines 808ff.

[7]Luke 2:41-51. Peter, James and John were often singled out from among the other disciples, for example, on the Mount of Transfiguration (Mt. 17:1-8). John was called "the beloved disciple," indicating a special bond of friendship with his master. See John 2:1-11; Luke 7:34; Matthew 23:37; Mark 4:35-38 and 6:34; Luke 22:44 and Matthew 26:38.

Chapter 2

[1]Benjamn Jowett, trans., *The Dialogues of Plato* (New York: Random House, 1937), I, 248-49. Quotations from Plato in the following section are taken from the *Phaedrus*, pp. 248-55.

[2]Alexander Roberts and James Donaldson, eds., *The Ante-Nicene Fathers*, I. In his "First Apology," Justin wrote of the way the Greek philosophers had been Christians before Christ, for they had lived "reasonably" (*meta logou*, "with reason" or "with the Word"). He equates the "reasoning" of the Platonic tradition in Greek philosophy with the general revelation of Christ as the Word (*logos*). "We have been taught that Christ is the first-born of God, and we have declared above that He is the Word of whom every race of men were partakers; and those who lived reasonably were Christians, even though they have been thought atheists; as among the Greeks, Socrates and Heraclitus, and men like them, and among the barbarians, Abraham, and Ananias, and Azarias, and Misael, and Elias" (p. 178). "I confess that I both boast and with all my strength strive to be found a Christian; not because the teachings of Plato are different from those of Christ, but because they are not in all respects similar, as neither are those of the others, Stoics, and poets, and historians.... For each man spoke well in proportion to the share he had of the spermatic word, seeing what was related to it. ... Whatever things were rightly said among all men, are the property

of us Christians. For all the writers were able to see realities darkly through the sowing of the implanted word that was in them" (p. 193).

[3]Roberts and Donaldson, II, 323. Clement expressed Justin's positive view of the Greeks even more clearly. He even wrote that their philosophy "justified the Greeks." He made quite explicit the comparison between God's leading of the Jews to Christ through the Old Testament law and his leading of the Greeks to Christ by this philosophy. "The same God that furnished both the Covenants was the giver of Greek philosophy to the Greeks, by which the Almighty is glorified among the Greeks. . . . Accordingly then, from the Hellenic training, and also from that of the law; are gathered into the one race of the sacred people those who accept faith; not that the three peoples are separated by time, . . . but trained in different Covenants of the one Lord, by the Word of the one Lord" (pp. 489-90).

With such a positive view of the Platonic tradition in philosophy it is not surprising that many Christians began to read the New Testament with many of the ideas of Platonic thinking in mind.

[4]S. Mackenna, trans., *The Essence of Plotinus* (New York: Oxford University Press, 1948), V, iii, 161.

[5]Ibid., 162.

[6]Ibid., 183.

[7]Vladimir Lossky, *The Mystical Theology of the Eastern Church* (Cambridge and London: James Clarke and Co., 1968), p. 25.

[8]Watchman Nee, *The Release of the Spirit* (Bombay: Gospel Literature Service, 1965). Nee writes, "One rather remarkable thing is that God does not mean to distinguish between His Spirit and our spirit" (p. 20). He makes even clearer what he intends further on: "Thus, the release of the spirit is the release of the human spirit as well as the release of the Holy Spirit, who is in the spirit of man. Since the Holy Spirit and our spirit are joined into one, they can be distinguished only in name, not in fact" (p. 21). He seems to suggest here that there is a union of being between the Holy Spirit and man's spirit so that the two become one being. This is contrary to the biblical teaching that God is never confused with man.

[9]Lossky, pp. 33-34. Lossky is quoting from Gregory of Nyssa at this point in his discussion of the Divine Darkness. He continues, "St. Gregory Naziansen, in quoting Plato without naming him ('one of the Greek divines'), corrects a passage from the Timaeus on the difficulty of knowing God and the impossibility of expressing His nature in the following way: 'It is difficult to conceive God, but to define Him in words is impossible' " (p. 34).

[10]Lossky, pp. 199-203. "The beginning of the spiritual life is conversion (*epistrophe*), an attitude of the will turning toward God and renouncing the world. 'The world' has here a particular ascetic connotation. 'The world is said by speculative examination to be the extension of a common name to distinct passions,' says St. Isaac the Syrian. . . . 'The world' signifies here a dispersion, the soul's wandering outside itself, a treason against its real nature. For the soul is not in itself sub-

ject to passions, but becomes so when it leaves its interior simplicity and exteriorizes itself. Renunciation of the world is thus a re-entering of the soul into itself, a concentration, a reintegration of the spiritual being in its return to communion with God." In such a passage we see the contrast between the mystical view of the Christian life and the biblical view very clearly. The New Testament tells us not to *leave* the world of human thought and feeling, but to renounce *sinful* thoughts and feelings. (Compare Jas. 3:13-18 where James defines what is earthly, that is, worldly, and what is heavenly.)

[11]Ibid., pp. 208ff. Lossky quotes Isaac the Syrian on this state of "spiritual silence" which is above prayer. "As the saints in the world to come no longer pray, their minds having been engulfed in the Divine Spirit, but dwell in ecstasy in that excellent glory; so the mind, when it has been made worthy of perceiving the blessedness of the age to come, will forget itself and all that is here, and will no longer be moved by the thought of anything." Again, compare the emphasis of the New Testament which encourages us to pray always with specific things in mind (Phil. 4:6; Rom. 15:30-32; Col. 1:3-4; 4:2-4; 1 Thess. 1:2). Note, too, how Revelation presents us as praising God *verbally* in heaven.

[12]E. Kadloubovsky and G. E. H. Palmer, trans., writings from the "Philokalia on Prayer of the Heart" from the Russian text *Dobrotolubiye* (London: Faber and Faber, 1951), pp. 33-34.

[13]Lama Anagariku Govinda, *Foundations of Tibetan Mysticism* (London: Rider & Co., 1960), pp. 18-24. A mantra is either a brief petition or a single word repeated as a "tool for thinking," a "thing which creates a mental picture." The purpose of the mantra being repeated and concentrated on is "to call forth its content into a state of immediate reality." Through the use of the mantra the individual is intended to discover a new dimension to reality, "a world within himself, opening up the vista of a higher form of life." The most well-known mantra is the Indian sacred syllable *OM,* which is used to "express what is beyond words and forms, beyond limitations and classification, beyond definition and explanation: *the experience of the infinite within us.*" This language communicates the same idea expressed in the Christian mystics; just as they used the Prayer of the Heart to get beyond a sense of themselves, to overcome experience of anything external or internal, and to enter a state of consciousness beyond subjectivity or objectivity, activity or passivity, so the Hindu mystic uses his mantra to pass beyond the categories of finite experience.

[14]William James, *The Varieties of Religious Experience* (London: Collins, 1960), p. 404. James writes, "This overcoming of all the usual barriers between the individual and the Absolute is the great mystic achievement. In mystic states we both become one with the Absolute and we become aware of our oneness. This is the everlasting and triumphant mystical tradition, hardly altered by differences of clime or creed. In Hinduism, in Neo-Platonism, in Sufism, in Christian mysticism, in Whitmanism, we find the same recurring note, so that there is about mystical utterances an eternal unanimity which ought to make a critic

stop and think, and which bring it about that the mystical classics have, as has been said, neither birthday nor native land. Perpetually telling of the unity of man with God, their speech antedates languages, and they do not grow old." This similarity ought to make the evangelical Christian stop to consider whether the mystical tradition in the church is biblical.

15Ibid., p. 441. James compares George Müller very unfavorably with the mystics, for the mystics write of their flight from reality into internal ecstasy, while Müller writes of his praying in faith that God would provide the daily needs of the orphanages and other works he established.

16Carl Gustav Jung, *Psychology and Religion* (New Haven: Yale University Press, 1938), pp. 4-7. Jung describes religion as "the term that designates the attitude peculiar to a consciousness which has been altered by the experience of the numinosum" (p. 6). "The numinosum is either a quality of a visible object or the influence of an invisible presence causing a peculiar alteration of consciousness" (p. 4). He says that all creeds or systems of belief in the various religions are simply "codified and dogmatized forms of original religious experience" (p. 6) and so the psychologist, "in as much as he assumes a scientific attitude, has to disregard the claim of every creed to be the unique and eternal truth. He must keep his eye on the human side of the religious problem, in that he is concerned with the original religious experience quite apart from what the creeds have made of it" (p. 7). Jung concludes, therefore, that all religious experience is equally valid as long as it has a beneficial effect. Even if the individual is practicing in the occult and has a healing experience, then he can know he has experienced "the grace of God" (p. 114). It is this total disregard of Christianity's claims to be the truth, and at the same time a preparedness to use Christian terminology, which makes Jungian psychology subtly dangerous and confusing. Faced with such an indefinite approach to language, Christians must be prepared to be continually asking people what they mean by the terms they use, rather than accepting religious statements at face value. Also, Christians must be prepared to present Christianity in such a way that we make clear that we are speaking about objective truth and not "religious experience" only. If we do not, we may be communicating precisely nothing as we speak to individuals who have a Jungian view.

17Morton Kelsey, *Encounter with God* (London: Hodder and Stoughton, 1972), on Jung, see pp. 102-21. Kelsey describes what he means by "God" and it is very clear that he has the same view of religion as Jung, as he later asserts explicitly. "Whatever name we use for the object of religious seeking, 'the divine,' 'God,' 'the numinous' or 'the Holy,' certainly refers to just such a reality as we have tried to suggest. The divine is that which has power and autonomy, gives meaning and purpose, and at least contains the qualities of our inner and personal nature" (p. 27).

18Comment by Larry Christenson on the back cover of *Encounter with God*.

[19]John L. Sherrill, in *Encounter with God,* p. 7. Sherrill writes in the foreword, "I met Jesus as an experience. I encountered His Spirit as an experience. Morton urged me to see these personal encounters in the broad framework of history and theology." We would agree that it is essential to see our personal experiences of Christ and the Spirit against a broader framework, but it must be the biblical framework, not the Platonic, or we will end up outside the Christian faith regardless of how powerful our experiences are.

[20]Nee, *The Release of the Spirit,* p. 24.

[21]Ibid., pp. 93-94 and pp. 24-25. Nee seems in these passages to be advocating a kind of detachment from life where the emotions are not involved at all. "If through the mercy of God, our outward man has been broken, we may be thus characterized: yesterday we were full of curiosity, but today it is impossible to be curious. Formerly our emotions could be easily aroused, either stirring our love, the most delicate emotion, or provoking our temper, the crudest. But no matter how many things crowd upon us, our inward man remains unmoved, the presence of God unchanged, and our inner peace unruffled" (p. 25). The presence of God with the believer in Jesus is a fact, not something which is dependent on our being able to keep our emotions at bay. We should note too that Jesus is spoken of as experiencing many emotions and Paul describes himself as a man of deep feelings (2 Cor. 2:1-4; 6:11-13).

[22]Ibid., pp. 65-74. "We are not first enlightened and then, with the passage of time, gradually brought into death. Rather we fall down instantaneously at the coming of light" (p. 78). Nee describes this enlightenment, or the breaking of the outer man, as the way to spiritual maturity. The confusion seems to come from his regarding man's spirit as unfallen. The spirit itself is always pure, having the nature of God, and so this pure spirit must be liberated by breaking the sinful outer man of thoughts and emotions. This is a very serious confusion, for the whole of man's nature (down to his innermost being) is affected by the Fall, not only what Nee calls the outer man. In fact the Scripture gives us no grounds for making such a distinction of the individual human being into inner and outer, or spirit, soul and body. There are one or two passages in the New Testament which speak of the dividing of soul and spirit (Heb. 4:12), or the body, soul and spirit (1 Thess. 5:23), but why should these be taken as physiological descriptions? No one takes such a verse as "Love the Lord your God with all your heart and soul and mind and strength" as a description of separable parts in man, but rather as an emphatic way of saying, "You must love God completely, with your whole self."

[23]Ibid., p. 89.

[24]Brother Lawrence, quoted in *The Release of the Spirit,* pp. 25, 28.

[25]Juan Mascaro, trans., *The Bhagavad-Gita* (New York: Penguin Books, 1962). Arjuna asks, "What is the work of the man of tranquil wisdom who pursues the goal of Yoga ('Yoga is evenness of mind—a peace that is ever the same')?" Krishna replies, "He whose mind is untroubled by sorrows, and for pleasures he has no longings, beyond passion, and

fear and anger, he is the sage of unwavering mind. Who everywhere is free from all ties, who neither rejoices nor sorrows if fortune is good or is ill, his is a serene wisdom. When in recollection he withdraws all his senses from the attractions of the pleasures of sense, even as a tortoise withdraws all its limbs, then his is a serene wisdom" (p. 53). Later Krishna encourages Arjuna to join in the "action of war" but to work "free from attachments," "free from the bonds of desire," "beyond what is done and beyond what is not done" (pp. 56-57). This is very similar to the passionlessness sought after by the Eastern Orthodox mystic which we referred to earlier in the chapter.

Chapter 3

[1]Kelsey, pp. 174-75.

[2]Ibid., pp. 180-81. It is clear in this quotation from Kelsey that there is a confusion between the unconscious part of the self and the Holy Spirit. See also p. 184 on the experiences which result from practicing inner silence.

[3]The New Testament term *flesh* means "the sinful nature." When Paul speaks of the battle between the Spirit and the flesh (Gal. 5:16-17; Rom. 8:5-9) he does not mean that the Holy Spirit is battling against our "bodies" but against the sin within us. He uses the term *flesh* in this context because our bodies are that part of us most obviously affected by the Fall and the curse in their subjection to sickness, injury, decay and finally death. *Flesh* and sometimes *body* refer to our sinful nature and how it affects our present human experience. We continue to have desires and thoughts which are corrupt and wrong because, though still God's image, we have a sinful nature.

[4]F. F. Bruce in E. K. Simpson and F. F. Bruce, *Commentary on the Epistles to the Ephesians and the Colossians* (Grand Rapids: Eerdmans, 1957), pp. 248-50 and footnotes.

[5]Nee, *The Release of the Spirit*, p. 89. Nee's stress on not putting confidence in one's own ideas is excellent, but it seems to us he goes beyond this, in suggesting that doctrine and its exposition are not helpful even if they seem to be helpful. He is, we suggest, bound to reach such a conclusion because his view of the self is so negative and because he sees the Holy Spirit working only in the spirit, not into the whole of the believer's experience.

Chapter 4

[1]Watchman Nee, *The Normal Christian Life* (London: Victory Press, 1961), p. 105. In the chapter on Romans 7, he suggests that *law* in Paul's writings always carries the idea of trying to do something for God. "God has certain holy and righteous demands which he places upon me: that is law. Now if law means that God requires something of me for their fulfillment, then deliverance from law means that He no longer requires that from me, but Himself provides it. Law implies that God requires me to do something for Him; deliverance from Law implies that He exempts me from doing it, and that in grace He does it Himself." Because he insists that this is the only meaning of *law* he draws the conclusion: "Nowhere in the N.T. are men of faith told that they are

to keep the law" (p. 107). In fact as we show later in chap. four, the New Testament does command the man of faith to keep the law (Jas. 1:22-25). Consequently, Nee concludes that the Christian is to stop trying to obey God: "Having at last reached the point of utter despair in ourselves so that we cease even to try, we put our trust in the Lord to manifest his resurrection life in us.... The sooner we too give up trying the better, for if we monopolize the task there is no room left for the Holy Spirit" (p. 111). In contrast to such a view of the passivity of the self, Paul commands us to work at obedience precisely because we know that in Christ God loves us and has given us his Spirit to strengthen us.

²Paul discusses the place of the law for the Old Testament believer in Galatians 3:23-26. The law was a pedagogue during the period from Sinai until Christ's coming. A pedagogue was one who kept a schoolboy under restraint. He made sure the boy went to school and studied. The law acted in this way to lead the Old Testament believers to Christ. First, it exposed sinfulness very clearly so that the Israelites could see the impossibility of trying to establish their own righteousness before God as a ground of acceptance and could realize their need for God's forgiving mercy. The law was given then to establish the principle that righteousness comes through faith alone. It was given to Israel not so that they might try to justify themselves, but that they might continue studying the promise to Abraham of righteousness through faith and that God would send a deliverer. The ceremonial law also served this same purpose in showing the Israelites (made conscious of their need for forgiveness by the moral law) that forgiveness could only come through substitution. It portrayed in the various sacrifices what Christ would do. The Old Testament believer needed the law's restraint and prodding because Christ had not yet come to fulfill the prophecies, the sacrificial system and the promise that God would impute righteousness to the one who believed in him. This is what Paul means when he says, "before faith came" (Gal. 3:23). He does not mean that justification was through works in the Old Testament. This was never the case, as he shows by referring to Abraham and Habbakuk (Gal. 3:10-11). Nor does Paul mean that there was no faith in the Old Testament. Rather he means that the principle of faith came into the full light of day when Christ, the object of the Old Testament believers' faith and hope, had come. Paul's statement must be taken relatively, just as his statement that Christ "brought life and immortality to light" (2 Tim. 1:10) cannot be taken absolutely for there are many promises in the Old Testament concerning eternal life and resurrection from the dead (for example, Ps. 23; Job 19:25-26).

Chapter 5

¹Gordon C. Olson makes this point in his discussion of God's moral government in his booklet *The Moral Government of God* (Minneapolis: Men for Missions, 1966), pp. 42-43, and also in *Sharing Your Faith* (Schloss Hurloch: Truth Press International, n.d.), p. 14. Olson writes, "Future choices of moral beings, when acting freely in their moral agency, have not been brought into existence as yet and thus are not fixities

or objects of possible knowledge. This applies to actions of the Godhead as well as to the self-caused actions of men." Olson says, then, that to say God knows all he will do is to apply "Fate to the Infinite. Choice is impossible without the origination of something new." Because he begins from his own idea of what moral government by God ought to involve, Olson then has to deny God's complete foreknowledge. (But, compare Jesus' statement in Mt. 10:29-30 and Is. 40-41 for God's rule over history.) His view also leads him to say that when God does predict what someone will do or what he himself will do, God then suspends his normal moral government and controls "the human will in the absolute sense . . . setting aside in such acts its normal moral freedom and accountability, and placing it temporarily under a law of cause and effect" (p. 15). Olson says quite simply that when God plans something, it means man's moral responsibility is set aside; and if man chooses, then God cannot even predict his choices. This is an excellent example of the problems that can result from beginning from a preconceived notion of what the Scripture must mean, rather than actually looking at what it says. Olson's view would mean, for example, that Herod, Pilate, Judas, Caiaphas and others were not morally responsible for Christ's death.

Chapter 6

[1]Paul's most powerful defense of marriage is in 1 Timothy 4:1-5. He says that "some will depart from the faith by giving heed to deceitful spirits and doctrines of demons," and among these he lists those "who forbid marriage." It is in the context of the validity of marriage that he says, "For everything created by God is good, and nothing is to be rejected if it is received with thanksgiving." See also Ephesians 5:22-23; Colossians 3:18-19; 1 Thessalonians 4:3-5; 1 Timothy 3:2, 12.

Chapter 7

[1]"When Scientists Play the Role of God," *The London Times,* Nov. 16, 1968, p. 1.

[2]See Paul Hazard, *European Thought in the 18th Century* (New York: Penguin, 1973), especially chap. one, "Christianity on Trial." He says, "Rich and weighty as were the legacies bequeathed to us by old Greece and Rome, by the Middle Ages, and by the Renaissance, the fact remains that it is the 18th century of which we are the direct and lineal descendants" (p. 7).

[3]Baron Von Holbach said, "There is but one truth, the truth of Science. Let man cease to search outside the world in which he dwells for beings who may procure him a happiness that Nature refuses to grant." Quoted by Rogers, *A Student's History of Philosophy,* 3rd ed. (New York: Macmillan, 1960), p. 365.

[4]Hazard, p. 7.

[5]Immanuel Kant, *Critique of Pure Reason,* 1781. See on this Rogers, op. cit., pp. 389-90. "Philosophy has in general not been content to stop with the endless process of phenomena in space and time. It tries to get beyond . . . this infinite regress to the ultimate unconditioned reality on which finite things depend, and by doing so to find a basis for those ideas in which it wishes to believe—God, freedom, immortality. . . . Is now this

attempt to understand in final terms the nature of real existence one that can successfully be carried out? Kant answers that it is not;... when we try to apply the categories of the understanding beyond the data of things in space and time—beyond the phenomenal world—we are involved in inevitable illusion."

[6]Alan Richardson, *The Bible in the Age of Science* (London: SCM, 1961), p. 50. In *Religious Thought in the 19th Century* (Cambridge: Cambridge University Press, 1966), p. 18, Reardon says of Strauss: "The miraculous he (too) regarded as an impossibility and the history of Jesus necessarily void of supernatural import."

[7]Adolf Harnack, *What Is Christianity?* (1900), trans. R. Bultmann (New York: Harper Torchbooks, 1957), p. 28. See also p. 26: "We are firmly convinced that what happens in space and time is subject to the general laws of motion, and that in this sense, as an interruption of the order of nature, there can be no such thing as 'miracles.' "

[8]Compare J. S. Bezzant, *Objections to Christian Belief* (London: Constable, 1963), pp. 82ff. "This outline of Christian doctrine has been so shattered that the bare recital of it has the aspect of a malicious travesty."

[9]See on this E. L. Mascall, *The Secularization of Christianity* (London: Libra Books, 1967), chap. five. A. Hanson, ed., *Vindications* (London: SCM, 1966), is also helpful as an antidote to the skepticism of much form criticism.

[10]See in particular F. A. Schaeffer, *The God Who Is There* (Downers Grove, IL: InterVarsity Press, 1968) and *He Is There and He Is Not Silent* (Wheaton, IL: Tyndale, 1972); C. S. Lewis, *Mere Christianity* (New York: Macmillan, 1964) and *Miracles* (New York: Macmillan, 1963); Colin Chapman, *Christianity on Trial* (Berkhamsted: Lion, 1972), 1, 9-30; (Wheaton, IL: Tyndale, 1975).

[11]The history of evangelical anti-intellectualism goes back a long way and is different in the United Kingdom from the United States. In the former, a division must be made between establishment and nonconformity. In general, however, it can be said that evangelicalism has never been a powerful intellectual force within the Church of England. A. O. J. Cockshut, in *Religious Controversies of the 19th Century* (London: Methuen, 1966), p. 3, says, "Evangelicals laid all the stress on feeling not thought." "Evangelicalism, although it numbered amongst its leaders, both clerics and laymen, a large number of educated and intelligent people, was never an intellectual movement. It was in some sort a reaction against the agnostic intellectualism of the 18th century. One can discern in the movement a sort of perverse pride in abandoning the intellect on the threshold of religion." So says John Marlowe in *The Puritan Tradition in English Life* (London: Cresset Press, 1956), p. 52.

There was, therefore, already a weakness with respect to the mind when the rationalistic onslaught occurred around the middle of the nineteenth century. (Note in particular *Essays and Reviews* 1860 coming so soon after Darwin's *Origin of the Species* 1859.) What seemed to happen then was a type of "sublimation": the energies of evangelicalism, rather than being devoted (at least in part) to making adequate response to this intellectual attack, were channeled into the worldwide missionary movement which by this time was under way.

Thus a division between religious and secular activities became increasingly obvious. A hierarchy was recognized, with missionary work and evangelism at the top of the list and cultural and intellectual activities at the bottom. Hence, the traditional Christian position to which the evangelical remained faithful became associated with anti-intellectualism, and philistinism, and later was derided as "fundamentalism." Sidgwick in a letter to *The London Times* in 1861 appealed for a refutation rather than a condemnation of *Essays and Reviews*. Of condemnations there were many; of refutations, few. Having failed to refute it, many before long denied the need to do so. The gospel had nothing to do with the human mind. Had not Paul said as much in 1 Corinthians 1?

In America the development of the same characteristics was largely the result of revivalism in the midnineteenth century, though, as in the case of the mother country, the origins lay further back. [See Richard Hofstadter, *Anti-intellectualism in American Life* (New York: Vintage, 1963), especially chap. three, "The Evangelical Spirit."] Some sections of American Protestantism resisted the movement away from scholarship and advocated an educated clergy throughout the nineteenth century and up to the present. As Hofstadter says, "It is doubtful that any community ever had more faith in the value of learning and intellect than Massachusetts Bay" (op. cit., p. 59). We do not imply that evangelicalism, either in England or in the United States, took a low view of the mind. Our point is simply that anti-intellectualism became a common feature in both. Happily, there are indications that it has been repudiated by the majority of evangelicals throughout the world in recent years. See also Harry Blamires, *The Christian Mind* (London: SPCK, 1963).

[12]On the development of these features, see F. A. Schaeffer, *The God Who Is There*, pp. 12-13 and *Escape from Reason* (Downers Grove, IL: InterVarsity Press, 1968); Os Guinness, *The Dust of Death* (Downers Grove, IL: InterVarsity Press, 1973).

[13]Jonathan Edwards (1703-58) *Select Works of Jonathan Edwards* (London: Banner of Truth Trust, 1959), II, 12.

[14]J. Gresham Machen, *Christian Faith in the Modern World* (London: Hodder and Stoughton, 1936), p. 70.

[15]Blamires, p. 117, "My claim is that if we did shift our ground, if we set about reconstituting the Christian mind, and began by taking for granted the authoritative, God-given nature of the Christian faith, and re-establishing in ourselves an unfaltering sense of the objectivity of the Christian truth, we should find it an exhilarating procedure."

[16]See F. A. Schaeffer, *The God Who Is There*, sections 3 and 4.

[17]B. M. G. Reardon, in ibid., pp. 20-21.

[18]John A. T. Robinson, *Honest to God* (Philadelphia: Westminster Press, 1963).

[19]Jack Rogers, *Confessions of a Conservative Evangelical* (Philadelphia: Westminster Press, 1974). Rogers suggests that biblical authority is

theological and ethical rather than historical and scientific. "Biblical scholars have long known that the first eleven chapters of Genesis are theological, not scientific information" (p. 126). He says that only the expert can tell the ordinary Christian whether details of the biblical message are actual history or simply theological meaning expressed in "cultural forms." The ordinary Christian can read the "simple story of God's good creation, man's sinful fall and Christ's gracious life, death, and resurrection for our salvation" (p. 62) but, the "vast body of supporting material" around this "central saving message" is, he says, too "complex and difficult," and so the scientific theologian must be called in to tell us the cultural form and background and therefore the meaning of the texts.

We should notice two things here. First, that one of the central tenets of the Reformation, as over against medieval Catholicism, was that the Bible is clear and can be understood by all—without experts. Secondly, as we saw above, Rogers himself says that the biblical account of the Creation and Fall is, according to the "scholars," theologically true rather than scientifically or historically accurate. This means, on Rogers' own admission, that in fact only the account of Christ's saving life, death and resurrection remains for the ordinary layman to be able to read and accept without having to worry that the scholar will suddenly tell him that this, too, is theologically true rather than historical fact. This leaves the ordinary Christian with a very small Bible!

One might ask, though, Why is the life, death and resurrection of Jesus above the experts' criticism? For some evangelicals it is not! For example, John Goldingay's article "Inspiration, Infallibility and Criticism" in *The Churchman* (Vol. 90, No. 1, Jan-March 1976) argues that it is not incompatible with the doctrine of infallibility and inspiration of Scripture to assert that John's Gospel does not "record *ipsissima verba,* or *ipsissima acta* of Jesus. Actual words and deeds have been preached, meditated on, translated, applied, and are perhaps no longer to be traced beneath the eventual text" (p. 13).

The same critical scholars who have said this about John's Gospel, have also said it about Matthew, Mark and Luke. The ordinary Christian may wonder whether he can trust his understanding at all as he reads the Bible. He will ask, What do the Gospels mean if they do not contain accurate accounts of the life, death and resurrection of Jesus?

Generally speaking, the debate among evangelicals has centered around the historicity and scientific accuracy of Genesis 1—11. What has been said above should suffice to make it clear that it has not stopped there and will not stop there. To introduce a hermeneutic (principle of interpretation) which depends on experts to tell you what is history or science and what is theology is like opening a dam which no one can stop. Eventually the whole Scripture is eroded, as it was in the nineteenth-century liberalism. Compare Charles Gore in England, for example, who at first accepted the view of rationalistic criticism that the Old Testament contained errors while he excepted the New Testament. By the end of his life, he was hard put to defend the New Testament against the inroads of the critics. Eventually Christianity becomes merely religious language describing personal experience, as it is for Jungian psychology. Against all such thinking we would affirm that the Bible speaks the truth in all areas.

Developments within evangelicalism during the past twenty years or so have made this issue even more acute. The same division between faith and reason has been introduced by some who call themselves "new evangelicals." In speaking about the Bible the term *infallibility* is still used but it is an infallibility limited to matters of faith and practice and not applied to facts of science. This has become a powerful influence within evangelicalism. Although it appears more conservative than the liberalism of, say, Harnack or Bultmann, it is just as damaging in the long run. [See A. R. Vidler, *The Church in an Age of Revolution* (Harmondsworth: Penguin, 1965), p. 195.]

[20]John Calvin and Charles Hodge treat the passage most helpfully in their commentaries on 1 Corinthians. Hodge on 1 Corinthians 2:6: "Paul in the preceding chapter vv. 17-31 asserted the insufficiency of human wisdom, and in verses 1-5 of this chapter he had said he was not a teacher of human wisdom. Was it to be inferred from this that he despised knowledge, that he was an illiterate condemner of letters, or that he taught nonsense? Far from it: he taught the highest wisdom. It is plain from this whole discussion that by the wisdom of the world Paul means that knowledge of God and divine things which men derive from reason. It is also plain that what he says of the worthlessness of that knowledge was in reference to it *as a means of salvation....* Whatever may be its value within its own sphere and for its own end, it is worse than useless as a substitute for the gospel" (London: Banner of Truth Trust, 1958), p. 33.

[21]Note the lengthy discussions Paul had with the Roman governor Felix (Acts 24:24-27). We do not know if Felix ever believed. Was he a "genuine seeker" or not? Paul reasoned with him regardless.

[22]This is not in conflict with Jesus' statement that we must not cast our pearls before swine (Mt. 7:6). He is referring on that occasion not to the person with whom we *can* discuss, but to the person who refuses to discuss and who shuts his ears against the gospel.

[23]J. R. W. Stott, *The Preacher's Portrait* (London: Tyndale Press, 1961), p. 49. He notes the evidence in support of this, briefly summarized as (a) the description of preaching in Acts as "teach," "argue," "dispute," "confound," "prove," "confute," and so on; (b) the apostles' practice of arguing and reasoning with men; and (c) the fact that conversion is frequently described as "acknowledging the truth."

[24]J. I. Packer, *Knowing God* (Downers Grove, IL: InterVarsity Press, 1973), p. 7.

Chapter 9

[1]See Roland Bainton's excellent biography on Luther entitled *Here I Stand* (Nashville: Abingdon, 1951), especially pp. 234ff.

[2]See Anthony Quinton, *The Listener* (April 10, 1969). "Quite a number of my reflective students . . . reject marriage as a morally undesirable infringement of human liberty. If two people want to live together, a

formal undertaking to do so is unnecessary. If two people do not want to live together anymore an undertaking that compels them to is undesirable" (p. 483). "When sexual satisfaction and parenthood were inseparably connected, the raison d'être of marriage was clear enough. Men, and women too, wanted sexual pleasure. But since women had so much to lose by pursuing it, they'd allow men to make love to them only on condition that the men undertook to support them and any children of the union.... This very straightforward equilibrium of interests between the two sexes must explain the very general prevalence of monogamy in all societies as a method of controlling sexual behavior. ... It [monogamy] remains the norm from which other arrangements deviate. [But] the assumptions on which this very practical justification of monogamy is based no longer obtain" (p. 484).

[3]One should also include the vast increase in the growth of divorce as an indication that our society views marriage in a quite different light than it was viewed, say, a generation ago.

[4]We do not consider it appropriate or necessary here to discuss the issue of evolution as it affects our view of original man, but we would like to stress that we know no reason, scientifically, why there should not have been an original couple, or even why the woman should not have been taken from the rib of the man. If creation as a whole is such a miracle, why could there not have been this particular miracle? Too much credence has been given to the theory of evolution and this constitutes the chief difficulty for evangelicals who find it hard to accept a literal Adam and Eve.

[5]See chap. six. One of the chief problems here is that people are not taught clearly from a young age that their identity is tied up not with marriage, but with personness. This is as true for men who do not get married (and who feel frustrated as a result) as it is for women. Being single puts strains on a person. But then so does being married, and this should be understood by young people. They ought not to be given the impression that if they do not get married their lives are useless. Christians should include this as a normal part of their teaching within the home and the church. If the understanding is clear that it is as *persons* that we are either fulfilled or unfulfilled, rather than as "married" or "unmarried," being single will not be so threatening. There are many situations in which a person is free to serve God and be fulfilled when single, which are not open to those who are married. (This is what Paul is dealing with in 1 Cor. 7.) But it is not just in philanthropic causes that a single person may seek to serve God. A woman is free to pursue a career and within it she may rise to a position of responsibility. The fact that she is placed in authority over men does not conflict with Paul's commands that women must not rule over men. Paul is dealing with the authority structure within the family and the church, not within the state or in commerce.

But the central issue in the whole discussion on singleness, of men as well as women, is the one which lies at the heart of this book. The single person is first of all a person *made in the image of God*. Therefore, he or she must live in the light of that, applying the same principles of human experience as those who are married.

⁶For a biblical view of woman see Gladys Hunt, *MS Means Myself* (Grand Rapids: Zondervan, 1972). This book deals very practically and humanly with some of the issues which have been raised by both secular and "biblical" feminism. On the family, see Edith Schaeffer, *What Is a Family?* (Old Tappan, NJ: Revell, 1975). This is an excellent book which all parents would do well to read.

Chapter 10

¹John Goldingay, "Inspiration, Infallibility and Criticism," p. 14. Goldingay suggests that there is theological diversity within the Bible and cites Paul and James on justification as an example. He suggests two possible resolutions to such a diversity. One, is a "theological situationalism"—the message is changed according to the situation. (This is obviously true but cannot be taken to mean, as Goldingay says, that there is a conflict of teaching in the Bible.) The other (following Käsemann) is that the later parts of the New Testament express "a different kind of faith, the institutionalized early Catholicism, from the dynamic of the Spirit . . . in Jesus and the earliest church" (p. 15).

What Goldingay is proposing here is that we accept the idea that some parts of the New Testament are further from the heart of the truth than others. One problem with such a view is that it then becomes a very subjective decision as to whether we will be bound by what the New Testament says. Some feminists, for example, have used this argument, saying that Paul's teaching on the equality of male and female in Galatians 3:28 is the "heart" of the message, while his teaching on authority in Ephesians 5:22ff is less than the "heart" and so we need not be bound by it today. We would assert over against any such view that there is no disagreement between Paul and James, and that such a principle of theological diversity destroys the doctrine of inspiration completely.

²Charles Hodge, *An Exposition of the First Epistle to the Corinthians* (London: The Banner of Truth Trust, 1958).

NAME & SUBJECT INDEX

BIBLICAL REFERENCES